FINAL FANTASY

AND

PHILOSOPHY

The Blackwell Philosophy and Pop Culture Series
Series Editor: William Irwin

South Park and Philosophy
Edited by Robert Arp

Metallica and Philosophy
Edited by William Irwin

Family Guy and Philosophy
Edited by J. Jeremy Wisnewski

The Daily Show and Philosophy
Edited by Jason Holt

Lost and Philosophy
Edited by Sharon Kaye

24 and Philosophy
*Edited by Richard Davis, Jennifer
Hart Week, and Ronald Weed*

Battlestar Galactica and
Philosophy
Edited by Jason T. Eberl

The Office and Philosophy
Edited by J. Jeremy Wisnewski

Batman and Philosophy
*Edited by Mark D. White and
Robert Arp*

House and Philosophy
Edited by Henry Jacoby

Watchmen and Philosophy
Edited by Mark D. White

X-Men and Philosophy
*Edited by Rebecca Housel and
J. Jeremy Wisnewski*

Terminator and Philosophy
*Edited by Richard Brown and
Kevin Decker*

Heroes and Philosophy
Edited by David Kyle Johnson

Twilight and Philosophy
*Edited by Rebecca Housel and
J. Jeremy Wisnewski*

FINAL FANTASY

AND

PHILOSOPHY

THE ULTIMATE WALKTHROUGH

Edited by Jason P. Blahuta
and Michel S. Beaulieu

John Wiley & Sons, Inc.

Published by John Wiley & Sons, Inc., Hoboken, New Jersey
Published simultaneously in Canada

For general information about our other products and services, please contact our Customer Care Department within the United States at (800) 762-2974, outside the United States at (317) 572-3993 or fax (317) 572-4002.

Wiley also publishes its books in a variety of electronic formats. Some content that appears in print may not be available in electronic books. For more information about Wiley products, visit our web site at www.wiley.com.

Library of Congress Cataloging-in-Publication Data:

Final fantasy and philosophy: the ultimate walkthrough/edited by Jason Blahuta and Michel Beaulieu.
p. cm.
Includes index.
ISBN 978-0-470-41536-8 (pbk.)
1. Final fantasy. 2. Fantasy games. 3. Video games—Philosophy. I. Blahuta, Jason. II. Beaulieu, Michel (Michel S.)
GV1469.25.F54F565 2010
793.93—dc22

2009008884

Printed in the United States of America

10 9 8 7 6 5 4 3 2 1

CONTENTS

Getting Started: The Alternative
Instruction Booklet   1

PART ONE

**BASIC CONTROLS AND UNDERSTANDING
YOUR CHARACTERS**

1   The Spiky-Haired Mercenary vs. the French
Narrative Theorist: *Final Fantasy VII* and the
Writerly Text   5
Benjamin Chandler

2   Kefka, Nietzsche, Foucault: Madness and
Nihilism in *Final Fantasy VI*   20
Kylie Prymus

3   Judging the Art of Video Games: Hume
and the Standard of Taste   33
Alex Nuttall

PART TWO

**PLAYING THE GAME–BUT WHAT IF IT'S
NOT A GAME?**

4   The Lifestream, Mako, and Gaia   47
Jay Foster

5 Gaia and Environmental Ethics
in *The Spirits Within* 61
Jason P. Blahuta

6 Objectification of Conscious Life Forms
in *Final Fantasy* 72
Robert Arp and Sarah Fisk

PART THREE
**ABILITIES YOU NEVER KNEW
YOU HAD**

7 *Final Fantasy* and the Purpose of Life 87
Greg Littmann

8 The Four Warriors of Light Saved
the World, but They Don't Deserve
Our Thanks 110
Nicolas Michaud

PART FOUR
SIDE QUESTS OF THE ENLIGHTENED

9 Shinto and Alien Influences
in *Final Fantasy VII* 125
Jonah Mitropoulos

10 Kupo for Karl and the Materialist
Conception of History 142
Michel S. Beaulieu

11 Sin, Otherworldliness,
and the Downside to Hope 151
David Hahn

PART FIVE
OTHER WAYS TO ENJOY THE GAME SO IT NEVER ENDS

12 Human, All Too Human: Cloud's
    Existential Quest for Authenticity   167
    Christopher R. Wood

13 Is the Fear of Stopping Justified?   185
    Kevin Fitzpatrick

14 What's in a Name? Cid, Cloud,
    and How Names Refer   195
    Andrew Russo and Jason Southworth

CONTRIBUTORS: Party Menu   209

INDEX: Game Tips   213

GETTING STARTED
The Alternative Instruction Booklet

Unbeknownst to you, the moment you first played *Final Fantasy* a "You Must Read *Final Fantasy and Philosophy*" spell was cast on you (we went back in time and bribed the programmers to put the spell into the first *Final Fantasy* some twenty years ago—and we hope you appreciate how hard it is to program a spell that will work in only 8-bit graphics!).

The "You Must Read" spell is a status-changing spell spliced together from Sleep, Confuse, and Fire. Sleep, because after staying up all night playing *Final Fantasy* and reading this book—which is really necessary if you want to enjoy the full intellectual richness of the *Final Fantasy* universe—you will need to sleep all day.

Confuse, because after you've read this book, you will never look at *Final Fantasy* the same way again. Questions like "Does Cloud really exist (or should we really care)?" "Are our Heroes really heroes?" "Should we fear our own stopping?" and "How should we think of and treat the nonhuman world?" will no longer be passing thoughts but all-consuming desires that compel you to quest after your own final philosophy.

And Fire, because this book will enflame your soul with a greater desire for *Final Fantasy* and all things philosophical.

Everything you need to achieve a greater understanding of *Final Fantasy* and transform your status is here: the Basic Controls, Playing the Game, Abilities, Side Quests, and Other Ways to Enjoy the Game. Mages, Moogles, Fiends, and Kefka, however, have been mashed together with the likes of Machiavelli, Marx, Foucault, and Kafka. The result, we hope, will launch you into your own philosophical quests of *Final Fantasy* and beyond. And, of course, your intellectual status will be forever changed on reading this book.

Your Party Menu consists of people like you, longtime fans who have spent years exploring the many worlds of *Final Fantasy*. Some of them, like some of you, have put off their education and careers in order to save a *Final Fantasy* world. Other began as gamers but became so enthralled with the intellectual depths and challenges of *Final Fantasy* that they pursued degrees in philosophy—perhaps the only truly fulfilling human activity beyond playing *Final Fantasy* and drinking—in order to keep their brains stimulated while waiting for the next *Final Fantasy* game to be released. Yet all of them still inhabit these worlds as Summoners, Mages, Warriors, and Thieves, dreading the day when it will be literally and figuratively GAME OVER.

PART ONE

BASIC CONTROLS AND UNDERSTANDING YOUR CHARACTERS

THE SPIKY-HAIRED MERCENARY VS. THE FRENCH NARRATIVE THEORIST: *FINAL FANTASY VII* AND THE WRITERLY TEXT

Benjamin Chandler

"C'mon, Newcomer. Follow Me": Interpreting Signs in the World of Gaia

Sephiroth hangs in the air before the imprisoned Holy. The time has come to save the world. The heroes are gathered: Red XIII, the giant talking red cat; Vincent Valentine, the demonic, shape-shifting former secret agent; Tifa Lockhart, the martial arts expert; Barret Wallace, the muscle man with the heart of gold, the mouth of a fisherman, and the arm of a, well, gun; Cid Highwind, the chain-smoking pilot; Cait Sith, the remote-controlled, fortune-telling robotic cat; Yuffie Kisaragi, the ninja; and you, the spiky-haired badass mercenary with a monstrous sword. But who will fight the final battle? The choice is yours.

Multiple playable characters allow players more avenues into a text. Roland Barthes (1915–1980) would call Squaresoft's *Final Fantasy VII* (1997) a writerly text because players take an active role in producing the game's narrative through their personal gaming experiences. Barthes was interested in semiology, the study of signs—signifiers (things that signify) and signifieds (what they signify)—and he believed that writers should fill their texts with signifiers, allowing the readers, or *consumers*, to interpret these for themselves and so *produce* the text.[1] Characters, objects, and places contain bundles of signifiers. The more playable characters a game has, the more ways a player has to interpret those signifiers, and the more texts the player can produce from it. This process depends on the level to which a player identifies with those characters.

Final Fantasy VII (*FFVII*) has nine playable characters, not including the brief flashback where Sephiroth is semiplayable, each with his or her own unique bundle of signifiers. They each provide a separate point of entry into the world of *FFVII* through the interpretation of their individual signifiers. These multiple entry points are one of the indicators of a writerly text.[2] Aside from these entry points, the *FFVII* franchise comprises multiple texts that combine to form the overall narrative: *Final Fantasy VII* (1997, RPG); *Advent Children* (2005, CGI movie); *Dirge of Cerberus* (2006, action/shooter); and *Crisis Core* (2008, action/RPG). There is also a collection of novels, a short anime (*Last Order*, 2005), a mobile phone game (*Before Crisis*, 2004), and numerous collectibles, including costumes, figurines, and an energy drink. These provide the consumer with even more avenues for entering the *FFVII* universe, and they multiply the number of signifiers within the series.

The characters in *FFVII* possess two different *types* of signifiers. The first type is built into the characters by the game developers, so we might call them *presets*; they are the fixed aspects of the characters: hair color, speech, age, and so on. Cloud Strife is a spiky-haired badass, Aeris is an ill-fated Cetra, and so on. These presets allow for only a limited set of signifiers, but the characters in *FFVII* contain psychological depth and therefore a significant number of presets.

The other types of signifiers contained within the *FFVII* characters are those that can be manipulated by the players. These we might call *customizations*, in that they are aspects of the characters that can be changed. Tifa might be a martial artist, but that doesn't mean players can't decide to make her a healer as well. Similarly, Red XIII can be a combination Magic-User and Summoner, whereas players might never use Cait Sith for anything at all. These variable customizations not only further increase the number of signifiers a character contains, they also allow players to alter those signifiers to suit their purposes. As Barthes would say, the game is a writerly text: players (consumers) can produce the text of the game for themselves, based on how they choose to interpret the signifiers they assign to each character.

There are limits, though. Customizations are themselves presets, in that the game developers decide what can be customized, what can't, and to what extent. I can't make my Cloud into a staff-wielding pastry chef; however, I can take the preset Cloud I start off with and make him into *my* Cloud, who will be different from anyone *else's* Cloud. James Paul Gee has already commented on this complicated relationship.[3] In his terms, my Cloud would become Benjamin-Cloud, and if Gee played *FFVII*, he would have a James-Cloud. Customizations multiply the number of signifiers a character possesses, based on the way players interpret the preset signifiers of a character and how they assign the customizable signifiers to those characters. This process requires the players to produce the text for themselves, making *FFVII* a writerly text.

A Malboro by Any Other Name: The Role of Identification in Interpreting Signifiers

Allowing players to customize characters multiplies the number of signifiers the characters contain and ways the characters can be interpreted within the text. It also actively involves players in producing the text through their interpretation of what the characters ultimately are. When I played *FFVII*, I interpreted Red XIII as a combination Magic-User/Summoner. By interpreting him in my own way, I was able to lay some sort of claim to him; he became Benjamin-Red XIII. Customizing characters increases the likelihood of player/character identification as players start to see themselves *as* their characters. When we finally defeat Sephiroth, we don't congratulate Cloud and his friends for doing a great job, but we take all the credit for ourselves. This identification leads to a greater immersion in the game world. A writerly video game like *FFVII* is one in which players construct the fictional world within the game by interpreting the signifiers contained within it. How players identify with the playable characters will affect how they interpret the bundle of signifiers that make up those characters. Similarly, how players interpret the signifiers within the game environment will affect how they experience the world and the events in *FFVII*—in other words, how they produce the text for themselves.

By "produce," I don't mean that players have to physically build the world of Gaia in *FFVII*; the game developers have already done that for them. As Henry Jenkins has noted, game designers become "narrative architects" who design and build game spaces in which players can experience narratives.[4] "Produce" means that players experience the fictional world by investing preset aspects (limited sets of signifiers) with meanings of their own. These meanings are focused through the identification process. Signifiers are contained within places (Midgar, Wutai, the Northern Crater), objects (potions, materia, weapons), or other characters or monsters (Marlene, Sephiroth, Chocobos), but how players interpret the signifiers within these game elements and the sort of text they will produce through them are dependent on how players identify with the game's playable characters.

Yuffie's hometown of Wutai contains a bundle of preset signifiers, such as "Wutai is the hometown of Yuffie," "Wutai lost a war against Shinra," "Wutai is home to ninja," and so on. For players, it may also contain signifiers such as "Wutai is the location of the Leviathan Materia" and "Wutai is where the All Creation item is that unlocks Yuffie's Limit Break attack." These signifiers are dependent on how players have come to identify with Yuffie and whether they have a character who is at least in part a Summoner. If they haven't been using Yuffie as a playable character, they may not complete the optional mini-quest necessary for acquiring All Creation. Similarly, if they aren't all that interested in summoning, they may see no reason to acquire the Leviathan Materia. Either way, the players' construction of Wutai will be different—if they spend much time there at all, it will be for different reasons. In other words, Wutai will signify different things to different players, depending on their interpretation of its signifiers and their identification with the playable characters—in this instance, Yuffie.

According to Barthes, however, signifiers are not solely dependent on character identification. Players can interpret the game world directly. Toward the end of *FFVII*, four monsters known as WEAPONs are released from the Northern Crater. The player fights two of these during the plot, but only one (Sapphire WEAPON) is destroyed in the course of the narrative. Whether the player destroys the other three (Ultima, Ruby, and Emerald WEAPONs) is a matter of choice. They are extraordinarily difficult to defeat; Ruby and Emerald are each stronger than the final boss in the game. The only things that you get for defeating them are items.

Some of the best items in the game, I'll grant you, but you can beat the game without them. More important, there aren't any consequences for the game world if you *don't* destroy them. The desire to destroy them comes from the player. Cloud or Tifa may wish to destroy them, but they don't force the issue. Identification with a playable character is not necessary. These mini-quests are only a small part of the overall game, however. They are a handful of battles among many, and they come toward the end of the game, when the players' construction of the game text should be almost, if not entirely, complete. Although players can produce the game text through a direct interpretation of signifiers, a true writerly text is dependent on character/player identification to guide the interpretation of those signifiers.

"Didn't Catch Your Name": The Player as Cloud

If identification comes from a combination of preset character traits and customizable aspects, most players will identify most strongly with Cloud because he is the one they spend the most time with. This means that players interpret the world of *FFVII* mostly through his set of signifiers, so the text they produce will be heavily influenced by Cloud's relationship to them. When Cloud and AVALANCHE blow up Mako Reactor No. 1, Cloud remains aloof, distancing players from the initial action and from AVALANCHE's ideologies. This does not mean that Cloud and the players have no opinions on the destruction of Mako Reactor No. 1 or of Shinra. Two of Cloud's preset signifiers, gleaned from the instruction booklet, are that "Cloud is an ex-SOLDIER" and "Shinra is bad." Players are influenced to produce a text in which what AVALANCHE is doing is "the right thing."

Players may find themselves on the horns of a moral dilemma when, as a result of Cloud and AVALANCHE's action, Shinra drops the plate onto Sector 7, killing everyone in the sector's slums and three nonplayable AVALANCHE members. Gamers and players might interpret this event differently. I use the term *gamer* to refer to someone whose only interest is beating the game, while *players* refers to those people who immerse themselves in the game world during the gameplay experience. The distinction between the two terms is completely arbitrary and is used only to distinguish between two approaches to playing video games. Gamers might not care that these people died—they are, after all, only interested in beating the game, and this is simply one part of that. Gamers interpret the signifiers contained within the game only in terms of how they contribute to the completion of the game. For them, the destruction of Mako Reactor No. 1 is the first feat in a series that needs to be accomplished to beat the game. The text they produce is not concerned with signifiers such as "innocent victims," or "senseless slaughter," but with more basic ones like "level one compete."

Players, on the other hand, do care about the destruction of the Sector 7 slums. They care because they are interested in such signifiers as "Cloud is a mercenary," "Cloud has a good heart," "Cloud's intentions are good," "Cloud is working with AVALANCHE," "Cloud's actions for the good result in the death of innocents," and so on. The text that players produce of *FFVII* is dependent on the process of interpreting these signifiers through their identification with Cloud: "*I* have a good heart," "*I* am working with AVALANCHE," "*My* actions for the good result in the death of innocents." The players' moral responsibility may be mitigated by further signifiers: "Shinra are the bad guys," "Cloud/I didn't decide to drop the plate," "Shinra should not have been using the Mako reactors in the first place," and so forth, but because players identify with Cloud, they bear the weight of the consequences of his actions—they produce the text most strongly through *his* collection of signifiers. RPGs rely on this sort of investment in the game world to provide the impetus for their completion.

Cloud's identity crisis partway through the game forces players to reinterpret the game text; his preset signifiers and the players' understanding of them are altered. Cloud learns that he was involved in one of Professor Hojo's experiments, that he was injected with Jenova cells and infused with Mako energy (like all SOLDIERs). He also learns that he was never a SOLDIER himself, and that he has taken on the identity of one of his friends, Zack, the sole playable character of *Crisis Core*. Players are forced to reorder their impressions of Cloud and the way Cloud shaped their experiences in the game world. The extent to which this is necessary will depend on the extent of their identification with Cloud. Gamers will most likely accept it as it comes: "Cloud has an identity crisis that spurs on the next part of the action." Players will need to reassess their interpretation of Cloud's signifiers and alter the way they have produced the text of the game up to this point. The result is a stronger level of identification with Cloud and a shift in perceptions of the game world based on an alteration of signifiers.

"Cloud . . . You Just Want Friends. Isn't That Right?" The Player as Party

The process of identification is more complex when there are multiple playable characters. This leads to a greater number of signifiers and a larger number of ways to interpret those signifiers. A distinction needs to be made here between party-based RPGs and strategy-based RPGs that may involve whole armies of characters. The games in the main *Final Fantasy* franchise usually have small parties of playable characters who work together to achieve a common goal. There is also a distinction between party-based games, where players take on the roles of those characters, and strategy-based games, where players become generals within the game controlling those characters.[5] Often players identify less with one specific character the more characters they have to control. Games that attempt to blend the party-based and the strategy-based include the *Suikoden* and the *Final Fantasy Tactics Advance* series, but in these games the majority of playable characters tend to have extremely limited preset characteristics, whereas a smaller group of playable characters are more fully fleshed out.

Final Fantasy VII is a party-based RPG. Cloud may be the main character, but the eight other playable characters provide further opportunities for player identification and signifier interpretation. Those who identify with Tifa from the outset may find themselves caring more about her relationship with Cloud, AVALANCHE, the Seventh Heaven bar, and Sector 7 than players who identify more strongly with Cid or Red XIII. This is because Tifa's love of these things forms a part of her character—they are some of her signifiers. Just as alternating perspectives in a novel can provide the reader with new vantage points from which to interpret a text, having multiple playable characters allows multiple ways of interpreting the game text. This is because part of what makes each character unique is the varied signifiers he or she contains.

Some players may, as I did, opt for maintaining a strong central party to the exclusion of the other characters. I became invested in Vincent and Lucrecia's story and in the happenings at Cosmo Canyon because I kept Vincent and Red XIII in my active party for most of the game. As such, I spent a great deal of time customizing their (and Cloud's) equipment and materia, while doing nothing with the other characters. This meant that I spent more time interpreting the preset signifiers contained within these characters and assigning them customizable signifiers of my own (Red XIII was a Magic-User and Summoner, Vincent a Healer and Command User, while Cloud was a Melee Attacker) to the exclusion of the others. This limited my experience of the characters I didn't play with to their preset actions within the plot, and as such my investment in and subsequent identification with them were lessened. The level of interaction and identification with a character will affect how, and the extent to which, players interpret that character's signifiers, which will have a significant effect on how players produce the game's text.

Aerith's death has a dramatic impact on both the preset Aerith and the customized player Aerith. Unlike Cloud's identity crisis, it doesn't force a reevaluation of the game text, but it removes one of the lenses through which players interpret it by eliminating one of the signifier bundles through which players produce the text. Gamers not invested in the game world or its characters may turn off the game at this point. The payoff in an RPG results largely from the players' ability to turn a weak starting character into a juggernaut. For gamers, this can be expressed as a simple formula: time (playtime) + effort (customization) = payoff (a more powerful character). This formula informs the gamer's interpretation of signifiers. When that payoff is taken away from the gamer, it results in a lot of wasted time and effort. Such is the case with Aerith's death, where the player's customization is nullified.

The extent to which Aerith's death upset players is evident in the numerous rumors that circulated over the Internet about the possibility of resurrecting her, as well as instructions for finding the glitch to see her ghost in Midgar. *FFVII*'s game developers were relying on players to be so invested in the game world that Aerith's death would not stop them from completing the game. This required the players to identify with characters other than Aerith, allowing them to continue interacting and interpreting the game text through alternate bundles of signifiers. It was therefore essential for the game developers to allow multiple points of entry into their game environment. These multiple entry points make *FFVII* a writerly text.

"Zack . . . SOLDIER First Class. Same as Cloud": The Player as Zack

Grand adventures usually start with the disruption of the natural order.[6] Prequels allow us to go back and experience what the world was like before the hero is called to arms. They are often tragic because they usually involve characters we know are dead in the contemporary setting of the original story, and we also know while consuming a prequel that something bad is about to happen that will spur the action in subsequent narratives. This tragic overshadowing influences the way players interpret the signifiers within a text and influences the type of text they will produce through those signifiers.

More experienced gamers may be able to correct me on this point, but to my knowledge *Crisis Core* is the first game where players know that the playable character has to die in order for them to complete the narrative. This means the game cannot be beaten. By drawing the narrative to a close, it can be completed, but no matter how well you customize Zack or how much time and effort you put in, you cannot defeat the final continuously spawning army of Shinra infantrymen that will be the cause of his death. Believe me, I tried. Knowing that it was futile, I still tried to fight for Benjamin-Zack's life.

So, why play the game? Although there are parts of the game that can be beaten, and monsters that can be vanquished, the ultimate payoff for playing *Crisis Core* is not in beating the game but in experiencing the world of Gaia through Zack's eyes and interpreting the text through *his* collection of signifiers (as opposed to Cloud's). Players already know what happened during the Nibelheim incident because they have seen it in flashbacks in *FFVII*, but in *Crisis Core* they get an insight into who Zack was and what caused Sephiroth's madness. This forces yet another reevaluation of the game text onto the player. Signs like SOLDIER or Sephiroth or the Turks take on new meanings, based on a player's interpretation of signifiers within *Crisis Core*. Even Cloud can be reinterpreted through our identification with Zack as we learn just how much Zack invested in him and how he shaped Cloud's bundle of signifiers. This makes mastering the original *FFVII* all the more satisfying because we now know that *we* have lived up to Zack's expectations. It is the ultimate expression of Barthes's writerly text—one that the consumer wants to expand by reevaluating the core narrative via another entry point.

"A New Life . . . Children Are Blessed with Spirit Energy and Are Brought into the World": *Advent Children* as Cathartic Dénouement

Advent Children is the first instance in the *FFVII* universe where players become entirely passive in a gameplay sense. I do not wish to enter the debate as to whether film audiences are passive or active, but viewers of *Advent Children* are passive in a gameplay sense—they cannot customize anything within the film. *Advent Children* provides yet another access point into the *FFVII* game world, but, unlike others, it makes no demands on the player's interpretation of the game text. It relies on viewers with preformed opinions about the world from their time as players. As a film, it doesn't have to construct its own imaginary world. Unlike the financially disastrous *Final Fantasy: The Spirits Within* (2001), which sought and never found a mainstream filmgoing audience, *Advent Children* is clearly targeted at fans of *FFVII* who have already come to identify with its main characters and who have already interpreted the signifiers within the text.

These interpretations may be proved false in the film, however, making it the least writerly text of the *FFVII* franchise. *Advent Children* moves away from Barthes's ideal, with its multiple signifiers open for interpretation, back to a more traditional text where the writer limits the signifiers and the consumer does not produce the text. The preset characters in *Advent Children* will probably be nothing like the characters a player has customized. Benjamin-Cloud loved his materia and never would have left them behind in the church to be stolen by the bad guys; Benjamin-Red XIII loved using the Knights of the Round summon, which the *Advent Children* Red XIII never does. This doesn't mean that a less writerly text cannot contribute to the larger writerly text of *FFVII*. Although *Advent Children*'s Cloud was different from Benjamin-Cloud, he still acted and spoke in the same way as the preset *FFVII* Cloud, so I was able to identify with him in the film. Cloud's set signifiers remained unaltered. It was only his customizable signifiers that were missing. Lacking these customizable signifiers meant that my interpretation of Cloud was more restricted, but *Advent Children* still provides another entry point into the *FFVII* universe.

"I Couldn't Stop Her. That Was My Sin": Exploring Vincent in *Dirge of Cerberus*

While acting as yet another access point into the world of *FFVII*, the mechanics of *Dirge of Cerberus* and the demands it placed on the players are as different from those of the original game as are the mechanics of the film and the demands it placed on its viewers. This game relies more heavily on reflex and gaming skill (the ability to push buttons in the correct order and with the right timing) than it does on developing a party and using it strategically. The first requires immediate responses, whereas the second requires more strategic thought, particularly if players adjust *FFVII*'s Active Time Battle system to give themselves more time to think and respond. These demands on the players' skill in *Dirge of Cerberus* influence the way players will interpret the signifiers within the game and allow players to produce a different kind of text from that produced through the original *FFVII*.

Not only does *Dirge of Cerberus* provide an opportunity for players to identify to a greater degree with a supporting playable character from the original game (Vincent), it also allows them to learn more about him and *his* view of the game world. We learn, for example, what Yuffie and Vincent were doing while the rest of the *FFVII* crew were watching Meteor fall on Midgar (as optional playable characters, they were left out of the ending cinematic of *FFVII*). *Dirge of Cerberus* aids in the pluralizing of the *FFVII* text by offering another access point and by moving beyond the scope of the original narrative. It multiplies the number of signifiers contained within the Vincent character, while providing new ways of interpreting those signifiers to produce the text.

"This Is the End?"

All texts contain signifiers, but in a writerly text those signifiers are multiplied to such an extent that the consumer of the text is forced to produce his or her own text through an interpretation of those signifiers. *Final Fantasy VII* is a prime example of a writerly text where the playable characters' preset signifiers are multiplied by the psychological depth of the characters and the players' identification with them. The ability to customize the characters in *FFVII* not only multiplies the number of signifiers they contain exponentially, but also requires players to interpret them based on how they are producing the text. Different texts will be produced by each person who plays the game, based on how the player identifies with the *FFVII* characters, and also how he or she interprets the signifiers within the various titles in the series. Thus, *FFVII* fulfills the ideal of Barthes's writerly text in a way that printed literature cannot.

NOTES

1. Roland Barthes, *S/Z*, translated by Richard Miller (London: Jonathan Cape, 1975), pp. 4–6.

2. Ibid., p. 5.

3. See James Paul Gee, *Why Video Games Are Good for Your Soul* (Australia: Common Ground, 2005).

4. Henry Jenkins, "Game Design as Narrative Architecture," in Noah Wardrip-Fruin and Pat Harrigan, eds., *First Person: New Media as Story, Performance, and Game* (Cambridge, Mass.: MIT, 2004), pp. 121–123.

5. Gee, *Why Video Games Are Good for Your Soul*, pp. 71–72.

6. See Joseph Campbell, *The Hero with a Thousand Faces* (London: Fontana, 1993).

KEFKA, NIETZSCHE, FOUCAULT: MADNESS AND NIHILISM IN *FINAL FANTASY VI*

Kylie Prymus

What are your values? They are peace, freedom, prosperity, wealth, and so on and so forth. So that any man who should, for instance, openly and knowingly act contrary to the whole of that list would, in your opinion, and in mine too, for that matter, be an obscurantist or a plain madman, wouldn't he?

—Fyodor Dostoyevsky, *Notes from Underground*

A Kefkaesque Beginning

"Kefka." Mere mention of the name conjures up the faint sound of synthesized laughter to the ears of those who have played *Final Fantasy VI*. The name, of course, is also an allusion to Franz Kafka (1883–1924), a philosophical writer well known for his twisted and unsettling perspectives on the world.

One of the most infamous villains of the *Final Fantasy* multiverse, Kefka Palazzo is also one of the most philosophically dense characters in video gaming lore. Despite his court jester attire and comic demeanor, Kefka is quite deliberate in enacting his goal of world destruction. He finds no meaning in the universe and sees the eradication of all forms of existence as his only reason for being. But is Kefka truly mad? Or are we simply unequipped to label a man with such wide-ranging homicidal tendencies any other way?

Kefka: The Man behind the Laugh

We first meet Kefka and the midi tones of his infamous laugh at the gates of Figaro Castle, where he has come in search of a strange woman named Terra. Unbeknownst to us at the time, Terra, a half-human, half-Esper hybrid, is one of the few people alive capable of controlling magic innately. Kefka is under orders from Emperor Gestahl to acquire her for the good of the Empire; whether they intend to use her for research or exploit her as a war machine is unclear. Even at this initial stage in the game, Kefka's sanity is questioned by the game's main protagonist, Locke. Later that evening, when Kefka attempts to burn the castle to the ground as a result of King Edgar's evasiveness, we witness his penchant for mass homicide.

What we are not told until much later in the story is that Kefka's behavior is the result of experiments done on him years earlier in an attempt to infuse humans with magical ability. Magic had all but disappeared from the world a millennium ago, when the three gods of magic ended a violent and bloody conflict with one another by willingly turning themselves to stone. The magical soldiers they had created, Espers, retreated to a separate part of the world and were gradually forgotten by humankind. Technology replaced magic as both tools of convenience and weapons of war until Emperor Gestahl began research into Magitek, a way to combine ancient magic with modern machinery. The only way to create Magitek or for humans to wield magic is through the acquisition of Magicite—the rare remains of deceased Espers. In an effort to end the Empire's dependence on rare artifacts for magical power, attempts were made to infuse human beings with Magicite. An adolescent Kefka was the first test subject, and it granted him the ability to wield some magical power, but it also effected a gradual change in his behavior, behavior that it is easy to characterize as insane and that we see for the first time at Figaro Castle.

We catch up with Kefka again later during the siege of Doma Castle. By this point even his own soldiers are wary of him, and after the general in charge is called away, Kefka takes matters into his own hands. Here the full extent of his murderous impulse becomes clear as he orders the entire castle's water supply poisoned, resulting in the death of nearly everyone inside, including some of the Empire's own troops who had been captured and imprisoned. "Nothing can beat the music of hundreds of voices screaming in unison!" Kefka yells in glee. It appears there is little left for us to do other than write him off as a deranged and archetypal criminal antagonist—the homicidal maniac.

Foucault: A Method to His Madness

There is no question that Kefka is homicidal, but is he truly mad? Enter Michel Foucault (1926–1984), a French philosopher who bore a striking resemblance to Uncle Fester. Underneath the turtleneck and the shiny pate, however, lay a man deeply concerned with the historical forces that have shaped modern-day structures of power. His first major work, *Madness and Civilization: A History of Insanity in the Age of Reason*, published in 1961, charts the history of the concept "*insane*" and how the label is applied to less desirable members of society as a way of controlling them. Although not initially a term of moral disapprobation, it has come to suggest a willful failure of not only the logical but the moral faculties, from the inability to be productive in society to the downright desire to engage in reprehensible acts.

Labels are powerful things. Forget the common mantra that "sticks and stones may break my bones, but names will never hurt me." Labels create social hierarchies and can invoke affirmation or condemnation, depending on their use. It is little wonder, for example, that Locke prefers to be called a treasure hunter, rather than a thief. Labeling people as "mad," according to Foucault, filled a space at the end of the Middle Ages once occupied by lepers. Leprosy was thought to be a disease not only of the body but also of the soul, as many believed it a curse from God for moral depravity. The construction of leper colonies gave the rest of society a sense of safety and superiority—no matter how downtrodden your lot, at least you weren't a leper! But constant quarantining led to the virtual disappearance of leprosy in Europe. A new group of outcasts was needed to give the general public peace of mind. The unfortunate targets of this restructuring were the insane. To isolate the "mad," fifteenth-century artists rendered them as cargo on a Ship of Fools, sailing just outside the city's borders with no direction and no greater purpose.

Prior to this change, during the Middle Ages, the common characteristics of madness were often thought to be signs of a veiled wisdom. Foucault noted that this older image of madness still persisted in literature after the Middle Ages—think of Don Quixote or Hamlet's grave diggers. Even the Heroes of our tale are no strangers to madness in their midst. Both the eccentric old magician Strago and the quirky but wise Moogles are examples of an older, more positive notion of madness. Even more telling for our purposes is Foucault's conviction that the transformation from insanity as veiled wisdom to madness as cultural fear begins with Christian views of the apocalypse. Biblical allusions to the human inability to comprehend the reason of God are taken to imply that those who come too close to such understanding will be driven insane. By the seventeenth century, madmen were feared because it was supposed that they were driven crazy by stumbling upon hidden secrets of the universe and the coming apocalypse.

If we take this symbolism and understanding of madness to heart, then the process of infusing Kefka with Magicite may have given him a revelation of "dark secrets and visions of the apocalypse"—knowledge that no human could comprehend. In the world of *Final Fantasy VI*, magic was controlled by three gods who removed themselves from the world, spawning an era of peace and tranquility that lasted a thousand years. With the rediscovery of magic, this peace is threatened. The fear of what would happen if the gods of magic should return gives rise to the notion of madness in the game, in much the same way that fear of the Christian apocalypse created the label of madness at the end of the Middle Ages. Kefka is quickly labeled mad because those around him fear the knowledge he may possess.

The Age of (Un)Reason

In the eighteenth century, the dawn of the Age of Enlightenment was heralded as the solution to all of humanity's problems. Foucault contended that nothing was more of a threat to humanity at this time than those who refused to employ reason—madness became the very antithesis of reason. Philosophers such as Immanuel Kant (1724–1804) even went so far as to provide us with purely rational justifications for morality. So, naturally, those whose capacities for reason were flawed came to be viewed as morally corrupt. Foucault marked this period as the "Great Confinement," or the birth of the insane asylum. The insane were locked away for the betterment of society, treated little differently than criminals even if they had committed no criminal acts. From this point onward, madness and depravity are inextricably linked. The marriage of these two concepts creates a set of familiar archetypes: the criminally insane, the violently deranged, and the homicidal maniac.

Players are quite comfortable giving Kefka such labels. Few of the protagonists attempt to reason with him, and certainly none desire to understand him. Any attempt he makes to persuade us of his position is ignored and invalidated. His arguments are routinely dismissed with a common logical fallacy, an ad hominem, or "appeal to the person." This fallacy involves referencing some aspect of a person's character as defective or undesirable, rather than criticizing the logic of the person's argument. A common use of this fallacy is to say, "You're crazy," implying that nothing of what you argue could be logically valid. Good reason, however, stands on its own; "twice two makes four" is a sound statement whether I am perfectly rational or certifiably insane. During the Great Confinement, however, there was no attempt to understand those who were locked up, just as we have no desire to understand Kefka. The insane were simply locked away and forgotten, "just" punishment for their perceived moral transgressions.

We are definitely justified in locking up Kefka—he is most definitely homicidal—but what evidence do we have that he is insane? There is a method to his madness, as Polonius would say of Hamlet. The poisoning of Doma was the most efficient and effective way of ending the siege swiftly and with a minimal loss of Imperial life. What is unreasonable about that? In fact, before the story ends Kefka amasses divine power and finds that there is no ultimate meaning behind the world's existence. He thus sets out to destroy it. If there is no purpose, no reason, then why should the world exist at all? This fundamental logic is the basis for the philosophical movement of existentialism, which we shall turn to shortly when we discuss the work of Nietzsche. Existentialism arose as a response to the Age of Enlightenment, proposing that logic cannot provide meaning to the world, so we must seek it elsewhere. If Kefka suffers from anything, perhaps it is not too little reason but too much. When he achieves the height of all rational power available to both humans and the gods, he suddenly finds no justification for life at all.

God Is Dead! Long Live Kefka!

The main theme of *Madness and Civilization* permeates all of Foucault's work: society has a desire for control and that which it cannot control, it seeks to dismiss. The very concept of madness has become a tool of dismissal and control. As we saw, labeling Kefka as mad is really just an attempt to ignore what may be a valid point of view. Now let's take a more serious look at how he acquired that view and what it entails.

After the massacre at Doma, we find Kefka at the Imperial Magitek research lab trying to coax magical power out of live Espers the Empire has captured. Learning that Magicite is actually the remains of dead Espers, he proceeds to kill them all, an act that disgusts his adoptive father, Cid, a perennial *Final Fantasy* favorite and the inventor of Magitek. Through a complex scheme of manipulation, Kefka convinces Emperor Gestahl and our Heroes to find and open the sealed door to the land of the Espers, whereupon he makes his final grab for power, killing the Emperor and draining all magical power from the petrified gods of magic. This results in a cataclysm that shatters the world and makes Kefka a god himself. In true arch-villain fashion, he builds a mighty tower within which he rules over all, doling out punishment at will and destroying entire towns that refuse allegiance to him. By all rights Kefka has achieved his goal—ultimate power and ultimate knowledge—and will be content to rule over all life for eternity.

When our varied band of protagonists finally manages to organize a resistance and scale Kefka's tower to confront him face-to-face, they find he has undergone an interesting metamorphosis. No longer garbed in jester robes or keen on snappy one-liners, he has instead taken on a winged, angelic form and his attitude is one of detached stoicism. The power and knowledge of the gods have changed him such that, to our horror, he no longer desires simply to rule over all but would rather destroy everything, creating a paradoxical "monument to nonexistence." By way of explanation, Kefka says that there is no meaning to the world, no reason that justifies its existence, so he will destroy it entirely. While ascending the tower for the final confrontation, our Heroes attempt to "argue" against Kefka and explain to him what gives their own lives meaning. Cyan lives to carry the memory of his family; Shadow has come to value friendship; Edgar wants to create a kingdom where people are free. These explanations fall on deaf ears, however, for Kefka is no longer subject to logic or reason. To be clear, though, he has not become unreasonable or illogical. Instead, Kefka's goals have become *a*rational—not contrary to reason but outside the domain of reason entirely.

Our Heroes' mistake as they attempt to sway Kefka from his nihilistic plan is in thinking that a meaning, a goal, or a purpose for life is something one can be convinced of. Although they each have motivating desires, desires are peculiar to each individual. They may hope that Kefka shares those desires, but if he does not, then no amount of logic will get him to agree on their importance. Most of us see existence as necessary, as an imperative. Kefka understands that this is not so, that existence is really only what philosophers call a *hypothetical imperative*.

A hypothetical imperative is something one should do or believe *if* one wishes to attain some further goal. In other words, it would simply be irrational not to follow a certain course of action if you have a particular end in mind. For example, I might say that you should unlock the secret characters Gogo and Umaro as you play through *Final Fantasy VI*. My reasons for this may be based on a desire for completeness or perhaps on the strengths these characters possess that make the game easier. These reasons assume, however, that you care about completing every element of the game or that you don't want the game to be overly difficult. *Hypothetically*, if you desire these things, then it is logically *imperative* for you to unlock these characters. But if you care for neither completion nor ease, then these arguments, regardless of how well I construct them, will not convince you. Similarly our Heroes, trying to convince Kefka that existence is imperative, invoke hypothetical desires that Kefka lacks. Therefore, without a reason that justifies the continued existence of the world, Kefka sees no alternative other than to effect its complete destruction.

Nietzsche: The Meaning of Morality in the World of Ruin

What a character. Kefka seems to personify exactly the sort of nihilistic, cynical, life-is-meaningless attitude that people might associate with, well, with philosophers! Existentialist philosophers, to be precise. This, however, would be a gross oversimplification. The existentialist movement represented by writers such as Fyodor Dostoyevsky (1821–1881), Friedrich Nietzsche (1844–1900), and Jean-Paul Sartre (1905–1980) more accurately expresses a belief that while life may lack an objective purpose, we are each born into the world with the ability to decide for ourselves what is meaningful. Nietzsche, in fact, recognized the potential dangers of a nihilistic outlook, particularly in a world that rejects God.[1] Yet he also saw in this the potential for an even greater justification for existence than philosophers had given before.[2]

Sporting a mustache that would turn Cyan green with envy, Nietzsche greatly influenced Foucault by employing the method of historically investigating concepts to better understand their modern meanings. Nietzsche called this process of outlining a *genealogy*, the most famous example of which is *On the Genealogy of Morals*, which explores the evolution of morality. Perhaps surprisingly, our understanding of Kefka can shed some light on the connections between Nietzsche's famous dictum "God is dead," the inherent meaninglessness of morality and existence, and the concept of the Übermensch or Nietzschean superman.

The moral history Nietzsche traces in the *Genealogy* documents the fate of two separate notions of "good": good in the sense of superior (good/bad) and moral good (good/evil). Long ago when the world was neatly divided between the noble, knightly, aristocratic class and the hardworking lower class, "*good*" was a term the nobility used to refer to themselves. They alone were fortunate enough to be endowed with intelligence, strength, and wealth. They looked down with pity, not hatred, on the lower class. The lower members of society were "bad" only in the sense that they were not "good." Their badness was relative, in much the same way that most weapons might be considered bad when compared to the Masamune—inferior, but not morally evil.

Kefka's relationship with the rest of humanity (and Moogledom) can be described this way. He feels no animosity toward our protagonists; after his ascent to godhood, he utters not a word of hatred toward them. The same cannot be said of our Heroes' opinion of Kefka. For most people, Kefka represents the living embodiment of evil. What is evil, though? According to the *Genealogy*, over time, especially with the advent of Christianity, the lower classes began to resent being looked at with pity and being abused by the nobility. So the downtrodden started a gradual change in the definition of the word "*good*." Rather than being a self-evident concept meaning "superior," "efficient," or "top-of-the-line," the lowly redefine good as the opposite of evil. So everything that the nobility cherish and hold dear is "evil," and "good" becomes its opposite. The nobility are seen as strong, so meekness becomes a virtue. The nobility have pride, so humility is now desirable. Poverty is a blessing that builds character. Compassion and altruism, which the nobility have no use for, at least when it concerns the lower class, become the cornerstone of the moral life. In time, these ideas take hold in the hearts and minds of all humanity and the distinction between good and evil is born. Nietzsche calls this transition in the meaning of good the *slave revolt* and the resulting moral norms, which exist to this day, *slave morality*.

So perhaps if we are quick to define Kefka as evil, it is only because we, too, think in terms of the slave morality. The scarred and chaotic world that exists after Kefka acquires his power is in many ways the direct result of the slave morality—Kefka punishing those who refuse to accept that he, as god, is good and that they are inferior, though not evil. If they would simply accept this state of affairs without complaint, without trying to rebel against him or label him, he would most likely let them be. They beg for compassion, but compassion is something that Kefka lacks, has always lacked, simply because it is a virtue created by those who lack power, and virtue is rationally unnecessary for superiority, or goodness, in the original sense of master morality.

Neo-Kefka: Übermensch or Failed God?

Nietzsche imagined that at some point in the future, the contradictory nature of the slave morality would become apparent and superior individuals would arise, creating a new morality of self-governance. Note that this new morality could not be called "better" or "worse," for what moral system can be used to judge moral systems themselves? Would we recognize such a superior person, an Übermensch, if we saw one? Is Kefka an Übermensch?

While Nietzsche may be best known for the dictum "God is dead," he did not mean the phrase as literally as many people think. The death of God signifies the end of an era in which the meaning of life is accepted unquestioningly from a religious (or other) authority that gained power during the slave revolt.

Uncertainty about what will fill the void of meaning created by the authority's collapse leads most people to close their minds to the thought. At one point Nietzsche has the character who proclaims the death of God (interestingly enough, a madman) give up and smash his lantern to the ground, declaring that he has come too soon and the world is not yet ready to face the consequences of a new, godless existence.

This lack of preparedness is the very worry that Kefka embodies, that without God there is no purpose or meaning to existence. Our fear is that a world in which God has been cast aside or replaced by reason alone is one in which the only possible end is nihilistic desire for the annihilation of everything. Kefka's failure to justify the meaning of existence shows us that this fear is still strong a hundred years after Nietzsche made us aware of it. If Kefka could not discover a meaning, despite his knowledge and power, what hope is there for the rest of us? Nietzsche wanted more than what Kefka could offer mankind. The Übermensch he described might initially resemble Kefka, but ultimately it shows him to be a false prophet. The real Übermensch is capable not only of overthrowing God and the old morality, but of overcoming nihilism as well: "This man of the future, who will redeem us not only from the hitherto reigning ideal but also from that which was bound to grow out of it, the great nausea, the will to nothingness, nihilism . . . this Antichrist and antinihilist."

Is Reason Really Madness?

Was Kefka truly mad? Or did he cause a change for the better in the world? At the conclusion of the game, amid the various happily-ever-afters and credits, we find a party of characters who have learned a great deal about themselves and how to live in the world. Although they may have lived satisfactory lives before, they were unenlightened and questioned nothing. The struggle against Kefka brought them face-to-face with the

negative influence of magic—of religion, control, and authority—
and tasked them with learning to live without it. Perhaps some
may think that an ideal world is one in which the gods of magic
remained frozen, or where a benevolent ruler usurped their
power and handed down a new meaning that would bring us
peace, prosperity, and purpose. If what Nietzsche said has the
ring of truth, however, then Kefka's rise and fall represent
the best possible situation. In the end, a world without magic
is not entirely blissful, it is not utopian, but neither should we
expect it to be. Our Heroes will struggle in this new world, but
their biggest struggle will also be the most rewarding, for it is
the banner under which philosophers have always served: the
struggle to find meaning itself when none is given.

NOTES

1. For more on Nietzsche's critique of religion, see David Hahn's "Sin, Otherworldliness,
and the Downside to Hope," chapter 11 in this volume.

2. For more on Nietzsche's response to the death of God, see Christopher R. Wood's
"Human, All Too Human: Cloud's Existential Quest for Authenticity," chapter 12 in
this volume.

JUDGING THE ART OF VIDEO GAMES: HUME AND THE STANDARD OF TASTE

Alex Nuttall

The Malboro appears in almost every *Final Fantasy* game as a very dangerous enemy, usually taking the form of a giant plant with a gruesome mouth and slimy tentacles. Its Bad Breath attack causes many status effects, including confusion, blindness, and charm. Yet, in a sense, the Malboro is artistic in its disgustingness. Furthermore, being confused, blinded, and charmed are the metaphorical states we are in when we first start to evaluate the quality of art in *Final Fantasy*. As players we are blinded by our biases, confused by inexperience, and muddled by poor senses. Unfortunately, we don't have a potion of remedy to overcome these ailments, but we do have the philosopher David Hume (1711–1776).

Hume argued that we can overcome our limitations to become good judges of art.[1] "Art" for Hume is a broad concept that included not only painting, but music, literature, dance, and so on. In this chapter we'll broaden the concept a little further to include video games. After all, who could deny that *Final Fantasy* is a work of art?

Beauty Is Not in the Eye of the Evil Eye

Before falling back on the tired conclusion that beauty is simply in the eye of the beholder, let's look at how we evaluate the artistic merit of video games. When we talk about general artistic qualities in video games, we applaud similar things. We think higher detail is better, as well as pretty visuals and interesting-looking 3-D models of monsters or characters. But when we look at a particular game, we may disagree entirely about whether those good qualities apply. I might find Sin's attack on Kilika Island in *Final Fantasy X* to be a great example of the Playstation 2 era, whereas you might see it as far too pixellated. Although we may agree on the general qualities of a good game, we may end up disagreeing entirely about any particular instance of one. Because of such disagreement, Hume believed it is natural to seek out a standard by which we can reconcile our various sentiments. *Sentiment* is Hume's term for our feelings or preferences.

It's odd that we should have any disagreement, though, as Hume suggested that beauty is not actually in objects. For example, the color red *is not* in an object. Such a statement might seem odd, but consider that when we see red, it is a sensation in our minds. The qualities that produce red are part of the physical world outside of us, but the experience of red is not. This is, of course, why people who've never seen color don't truly understand what it is. The beautiful rendering of Sin in *Final Fantasy X* is not in the image of Sin. The object "Sin," depicted as a giant floating creature, is just digital information translated into various wavelengths of light. It's hard to see where beauty would be in that object, and all art "objects" can be similarly broken down in terms of their physical components.

The next obvious place to look for beauty, then, is in the beholder—the person who sees the beauty. While Hume agreed, as a metaphysical point, that beauty is in the eye of the beholder, we should be cautious of misinterpreting what he took this view to mean.[2] When we say, "Beauty is in the eye of the beholder," it is usually to end disputes or conversations about whether something is beautiful. If I say that *Final Fantasy VIII*'s gun-swords are tacky and look silly, and you disagree and say, "Beauty is in the eye of the beholder," then there's not any more conversation to be had about the gun-swords—we simply take it that beauty is relative to each person. Hume, however, did not want us to end the conversation. While beauty may ultimately be in how we perceive an object, there does seem to be a strong connection between the object and what we perceive as beautiful, and without this connection we would be unable to have any standard of taste.

Could Cloud Strife Beat Superman in a Fight?

If beauty is not in objects, then it seems that all of our senti-ments would be equal—no one's sentiments would be better or worse than another person's. Sentiments, taken by them-selves, are neither right nor wrong. When we see the color red, our experience of red is neither right nor wrong—it just is. So why do we ever bother with disagreements about art? If it is, at root, as subjective as we've been discussing, there is no disagreement to be had. If I like chocolate ice cream and you like vanilla and you dislike chocolate and I dislike vanilla, there doesn't seem to be anything more to say about our preferences other than acknowledging them—and then buying and eating the ice cream we each like.

But Hume suggested that disagreements may arise from considering two artworks that are vastly different in quality. Let's compare *Final Fantasy VII* and its hero, Cloud Strife, with

Superman 64 and its hero, Superman. Cloud Strife is great with a sword, has special *limit break* powers, and, despite his identity problems, is an accomplished hero. Superman is insanely powerful and can do almost anything. In a battle, Superman would almost certainly win (unless Materia is actually kryptonite, in which case Cloud's chances of victory would be much greater). But what would happen in a fight between their respective video games? Those familiar with both games will immediately see a clear winner: *Final Fantasy VII*. This is because *Superman 64* is, by the estimation of many, a broken game. *Final Fantasy VII* is not only a working game, it is a game that is praised, is often discussed, and ranks highly in the history of video games. Is saying that *Superman 64* is a better game than *Final Fantasy VII* just as reasonable as saying the opposite? Keep in mind that the question is not whether someone likes or enjoys *Superman 64* (although it's hard to see how one can enjoy a broken game), but whether it is better than *Final Fantasy VII*. I think most of us would agree that there is little room for disagreement here—*Final Fantasy VII's* superiority is not simply a matter of what we *prefer*. We seem to recognize that there are differences of quality between works, and we don't always treat them as simply different flavors of ice cream. Now, do we bite the bullet and say that all of our disagreements are mistaken, or do we try to both explain how beauty is a subjective experience and maintain that we are still able to objectively assess its value?

The Sea Devil's in the Details

Like *Final Fantasy VII*, most of the games in the *Final Fantasy* series seem to be of higher quality than many other games that are available. Its full-motion videos, such as Bahamut's attack on Alexandria in *Final Fantasy IX*, are expertly rendered and awe-inspiring. Its stories are well told, emotionally gripping, and coherent. For example, Cecil the Dark Knight's path in

Final Fantasy IV to become a Paladin at Mt. Ordeals still gives me goose bumps. Interesting characters, plots, and art design are found throughout the *Final Fantasy* series. The excellent quality of these characteristics does not seem to simply be our subjective preference for them. But if they aren't subjective preferences, then what are these qualities? They can't be in the object, as we've already pointed out, at least not completely. Yet there does seem to be something in objects that excites particular perceptions. These perceptions have a strong relationship to certain qualities in the object.

Hume's description of a scene from *Don Quixote* shows us that there is more going on than simply our subjective experience of beauty.[3] In this scene, two wine connoisseurs taste wine from a barrel that is believed to be of excellent quality. They both judge it to be good, but one detects a hint of leather, the other a hint of iron. Later it is discovered that at the bottom of the barrel of wine, there is an iron key with a leather thong. Good judges, like these wine connoisseurs, can detect very small variations in a work. Although beauty is a perception, it does not seem to be entirely accidental. Our perceptions of beauty are affected by properties in the object that can either detract, like iron and leather, or add to the experience.

An unfortunate side effect of this view is that we are not all able to become good judges of art. Some of us will simply not have the perceptual acuity to notice such detail. But is noticing every detail always best for judging art? Often, artists will have a lot of detail in their works, and the art is best appreciated when these details are noticed. Not all art is about the details, however. Some art is best observed without excessive attention to its specifics. Hume would claim that focusing on these specifics brings the worth of a work down. Or, more precisely, he would say that good judges would agree that the specifics can detract from, rather than add value to, a work. Again, it's not obvious that Hume is right here. Sometimes the rough edges of a work add to the experience of it.

Brewing a *Remedy*: Qualities of Good Judges

In order to be good judges, Hume argued that we need "a perfect serenity of mind, a recollection of thought, a due attention to the object; if any of these circumstances be wanting, our experiment will be fallacious, and we shall be unable to judge of the catholic and universal beauty."[4] We need serene minds so that our moods don't influence our judgment. We must be able to carefully recollect the art in question so that we don't make mistakes in asserting what the art contains, and we must pay attention to details and be able to notice the nuance and subtlety in the art, or we will again fail to judge appropriately. In other words, we start out as if breathed on by the Malboro. We are confused, blinded, and charmed, and we need to alleviate each of these curses in order to judge well.

First, we need to gain experience in viewing art. Hume didn't suggest that we battle monsters to do this, however. We need to view different works of art, but not only that, we should engage in repeat viewings of the same works. In the *Final Fantasy* games, we often find ourselves engaged in battling Imps, Flans, and Chimeras multiple times and developing strategies to deal with them. Hume said we should do the same with art so that we are not charmed into thinking that a lower-quality work is a higher-quality one. More specifically, experience helps us avoid being seduced by art that, as Hume put it, is "florid and superficial." That is, art that seems pleasing at first but eventually is found to be sorely lacking in quality.

One reason Hume thought that we need to experience a lot of the art we are planning on judging is that we can't be fair judges of the art if we don't know what has been done with it before. It would be like trying to judge the whole *Final Fantasy* series by only playing any of the Crystal Chronicles games. Not that the Crystal Chronicles games are bad games; they simply are not representative of the series. *Final Fantasy* games are fairly diverse, even when they share many of the same elements—like Chocobos, Malboros, and status effects. The basic point is that we need to be aware of what has been done in an art medium before we can fairly judge a work in that medium. We might think something is great, only to find out that it has been done and redone many different ways, and perhaps it has been better done by someone else.

Viewing things may give us experience, but those experiences need to mean something if we are going to be good judges. As Hume stated, "By comparison alone we fix the epithets of praise or blame, and learn how to assign the due degree of each."[5] We need to compare and contrast the art we encounter. What are the qualities that separate games like *Final Fantasy* from other games? What makes *Final Fantasy VI* different from *Final Fantasy VII*? If one is better than the other, how do we explain this? This is the sort of process Hume had in mind when he said that we need to compare the art we view. By comparing, we refine our sensibilities and improve our insight into the qualities that make art succeed or fail. Once we start viewing art this way, we are well on our way to becoming good critics, but we are not there yet.

Charmed by Bias

If we were simply machines, like Warmech, experience and comparison would be enough for us to be good judges. Okay, so Warmech would probably just blast any art put in front of it. But we are different from Warmech: not only do we like looking at art, but we also suffer from particularly human limitations. The biggest limitation we have to deal with in judging art is bias. If we are biased or prejudiced, we can't accurately evaluate the relations of the parts of an artwork and how these relations bear on the work as a whole. In order to check the influence of bias and prejudice, we must employ *reason* in judging art. The careful use of reason throughout judging allows us to recognize when and where biases creep in and gives us strategies for eliminating them from our final judgments about the quality of a work of art. In role-playing games, I have a preference for sword fighters, which is fortunate because so many of *Final Fantasy's* lead characters are sword fighters (Cloud Strife, Tidus, Cecil, and so on). But this does not prevent me from recognizing the awesome power of a black-magic user's Fire spell or Odin summoning. Reason is a remedy against bias in gaming, as well as in judging.

Confused by Culture and Blinded by Our Dispositions

When we view art from other cultures or time periods, we need to keep in mind for whom the art was created and when. We can't adopt a perspective antithetical to the audience that the art was intended for. Take the first *Final Fantasy*, for instance. By today's standards, *Final Fantasy I* looks fairly dated, its story is very linear, and it is less emotionally involving than more recent installments in the series. But judging *Final Fantasy I* by today's standards would be very unfair because the game was produced without the technological advances we have now for an audience that was substantially younger demographically, in a medium (video games) that was still in its infancy.

The Malboro's curse of blindness still afflicts us, even with the eye drops of reason. Although reason can deal with many types of biases, some level of bias is inescapable simply because we are human. To deal with our more fundamental biases, such as how we were raised or our idiosyncratic dispositions, we can only recognize that we have them and take them into account whenever possible. Hume believed that these biases are innocent and natural because they don't completely impede the ability to judge art and there is no way to fully eliminate them. By making sure that our assessment of art is about the art itself and not about what our mood happened to be or what the weather was like, we can avoid most other bias that would undermine our ability to judge.

In this way we walk a fine line between our biases and the feelings that arise from the experience of art. We'll never be quite sure exactly whether the feelings arose because we witnessed something in the art or because we harbor some bias or predisposition to react in a particular manner. One thing we can do to sort out these feelings is to pay attention to whether we have some reason to explain a feeling—a reason that is founded in the work. If we don't have a reason founded in the work (or at least more than tangentially related to it), then the feeling may have simply arisen from some bias that we have. As Hume made clear, a focus on reasons helps us to stay vigilant against our errant emotions.

Our assessments should be focused on what makes the art good or bad and should not involve incidental, ancillary, or accidental elements. These elements need to be ruled out and accounted for in our final judgment. This is not to say, however, that we should approach art with a cold and calculating detachment. Doing so would be a failure to truly appreciate the art, because we would be preventing ourselves from feeling the emotions that the artist was expressing or that we get as a result of experiencing the art. That is, we should not be playing video games like *Final Fantasy* as merely the progression of some pixels on a screen; we should experience the game, and this includes relating to the characters and empathizing with their situation.

Hume made two other important points about human dispositions. The first is about the relationship between art and morality. According to Hume, if a work does not appropriately deal with an immoral act, then it is permissible for a judge to dismiss it out of hand. Consider, for instance, if Cecil, the hero of *Final Fantasy IV*, ended the world instead of saving it or committed gratuitously evil acts along the way. Events like these in a story would be enough to dismiss the game completely and nullify its artistic value. Although we wouldn't endorse Cecil's actions, it would be rash to immediately dismiss *Final Fantasy IV* solely on that basis. The rest of the game is otherwise excellent and deserves a fair assessment, despite the moral failings of our imaginary Cecil. Thus, Hume may have been a bit too quick on this point.

The second point about human dispositions that Hume addressed concerns religion. We should not judge a work based on its religious point of view. This follows Hume's discussion of the importance of adopting the perspective of the audience for which the artwork is intended. For instance, if Chris the Christian plays any *Final Fantasy* game and objects to it because its characters are not Christian and the game contains a world where multiple gods exist, then Chris has violated one of the rules of a good judge. He is not adopting an unbiased perspective from which to judge the game. There is a caveat, however. If the use of religion in the work promotes something immoral, then we can dismiss the work summarily.

Is Hume's Airship Flying in Circles?

Unfortunately, there are two problems with Hume's theory that we can't so easily forgive. Both deal with the confusion about how works that have stood the test of time, such as masterpieces, are related to good judges. The first problem is a worry about which of these is the real standard: masterpieces or good judges? The second problem is one of circularity: if good judges train with masterpieces to become good judges, and what counts as a masterpiece is determined by good judges, then there's a vicious circularity in Hume's theory. His airship isn't taking us anywhere. The relationship between good judges and masterpieces is unclear, but it's not fatal to Hume's theory.

To answer the first problem, it seems fairly clear that Hume meant for good judges to be the standard of taste, even while he assigned an important role to masterpieces. Hume focused on good judges and said that the joint verdict of critics is the standard of taste.[6] Also, masterpieces, by themselves, can't inform us on how to evaluate art, because simply comparing a work to a masterpiece would only give us the ability to see how alike the two pieces are. But we don't want new works to just be like masterpieces. New artworks should be original and special in their own right. It's premature to say that *Final Fantasy VII* is a masterpiece, but as far as video games go, it's pretty close. Yet we don't want games to simply mimic what *Final Fantasy VII* did. We want them to develop new techniques, higher graphical detail, and new, original stories.

Good judges, then, gain their experience by examining masterpieces and working to understand the reasons why they've stood the test of time. After refining their sensibilities on these masterpieces, they can then cast their net wider and start to evaluate art in general. By putting good judges and masterpieces in the right relationship, we have also found a solution to the problem of circularity. Because good judges aren't dependent on masterpieces to become good judges, but instead on an understanding of why masterpieces have been given their stature, there is no longer a vicious circularity. With this solution, we've put Hume's airship back on course.[7]

Taking Care of Bad Breath

In order to be good judges, we need "strong sense, united to a delicate sentiment, improved by practice, perfected by comparison, and cleared of all prejudice." This "alone entitle[s] critics to this valuable character; and the joint verdict of such, wherever they are to be found, is the true standard of taste and beauty."[8] Whether we ultimately agree with Hume's judges being the standard of taste, his prescription for being a good judge of art is good, no matter which theory you deem best.

It's unfortunate that the artistic value of *Final Fantasy* games (and video games in general) is largely ignored. Luckily, more and more people are seeing games as a meaningful pastime. If you have an interest in being a good judge of video games, every game you play can help you along that path. It takes careful analysis of each game you play, research of critical reviews of the game, and patient reflection. But that work is very rewarding—more rewarding, even, than defeating the Malboro! Not only do you get the joy of playing great games like the *Final Fantasy* series, but you also get the added benefit of refining your tastes, sharpening your thinking, and increasing your cultural awareness. And because artistic elements are often not medium-specific, you might find yourself using your newfound skills in judging movies, TV shows, books, and music. In no time at all, you'll clear up that Bad Breath!

NOTES

1. David Hume, "Of the Standard of Taste," in Stephen David Ross, ed., *Art and Its Significance: An Anthology of Aesthetic Experience* (Albany: SUNY, 1994), p. 87.

2. Metaphysics is the branch of philosophy concerned with the ultimate nature of reality. In this case, it is the ultimate nature of reality, according to Hume, that beauty is a perception and not a quality of objects in and of themselves.

3. Hume, "Of the Standard of Taste," p. 83.

4. Ibid., 82.

5. Ibid., 85.

6. Ibid., 87.

7. For a more detailed discussion of the arguments in this section, see Jerrold Levinson, "Hume's Standard of Taste: The Real Problem," in *The Journal of Aesthetics and Art Criticism* 60, no. 3 (Summer 2002): 227–238.

8. Hume, "Of the Standard of Taste," p. 87.

PART TWO

PLAYING THE GAME—BUT WHAT IF IT'S NOT A GAME?

THE LIFESTREAM, MAKO, AND GAIA

Jay Foster

Tapping the Lifestream

The specter of ecological apocalypse is nothing new to science fiction and fantasy. The original *Mad Max* (1979) portrayed an impoverished future brought to the brink of lawlessness by resource shortages, mainly oil. Likewise, *Blade Runner* (1982) envisioned a dismal and polluted future for the Earth after a runaway human population has rapaciously consumed all available natural resources. But the ecological apocalypse leitmotif is given a distinct, if not unique, twist in *Final Fantasy VII* (1997). In this installment of *Final Fantasy*, we are introduced to the Lifestream, a green-white fluid that is the source of all planetary life. When a person is born, energy is taken from the Lifestream, and when he or she dies, the Lifestream is replenished with the person's energy in the form of his or her knowledge and memories. The Lifestream, however, can also be artificially extracted and used, with potentially devastating consequences.

The same energy that makes the cycle of life and death is also tapped for magical and mundane power. Mako, energy extracted from the Lifestream, can be crystallized into Materia. And Materia, in turn, is the source of all magical power. It allows characters to cast spells; it gives weapons and armor special properties, and it can be used to summon creatures to help in battle. While Mako can be extracted in small quantities by natural processes, it can also be artificially extracted from the planet by Mako reactors. Artificially extracted Mako powers the mundane technologies, from cell phones to lights, which make life comfortable for the planet's human inhabitants. Everyday technological comforts come at a high environmental cost, however. The artificial extraction of energy from the Lifestream destroys the environment around the Mako reactor. Furthermore, the artificially extracted Mako never returns to the Lifestream—when it is used, it is completely consumed—and so the Lifestream is gradually depleted. And as the Lifestream is depleted, so is the capacity of the planet to support life.

Mako in the world of *Final Fantasy* bears more than a passing resemblance to fossil fuels in the real world, such as crude oil and coal. Mako is extracted from under the crust of the planet, whereas fossil fuels are mined or pumped from the ground. Mako is formed from the life of the planet, while fossil fuels have been formed from the preserved remains of plants that lived millions of years ago. Mako is the main source of energy to power the technology of the *Final Fantasy* world, whereas fossil fuels, directly or indirectly, power much (but not all) of our modern technological society. The extraction of Mako has serious environmental consequences: the sites of Mako extraction wither and die, and the use of Mako depletes the Lifestream. Similarly, the use of fossil fuels has significant environmental consequences: drilling for oil and mining coal often harms local ecologies, while burning fossil fuels releases carbon dioxide and other gases that contribute to global climate change. Indeed, much as in our world, in the world of *Final Fantasy* Mako reactors are run by a dark and powerful corporation (the Shinra Electric Power Company) that is the target of ecoterrorists (AVALANCHE).

Mako and fossil fuels have some common features, but they are clearly not the same thing. In its Materia form, Mako is used for spell casting and to add magical properties to weapons and armor. Fossil fuels can do neither of these things, of course. Nevertheless, the obvious conceptual similarities between Mako and fossil fuels invites us to think about the ecological concepts that inform the world of *Final Fantasy* in an effort to, perhaps, better understand the ecological concepts we use in the real world.

So, what can the ecological concepts used in *Final Fantasy* show us about the ecological concepts we use in the day-to-day world? To tackle this question, we need to do the philosophical work of *conceptual analysis.* Philosophers have different techniques for analyzing concepts, but, for the most part, the work involves taking a concept and either discovering the concepts that make it up or attempting to clarify the concept by comparing it with other concepts.

The following is a short exercise in conceptual analysis. We will attempt to clarify the concept of "the Lifestream," which appears in the game *Final Fantasy VII* but is more prominent in the *Final Fantasy* movies *The Spirits Within* (2001) and *Advent Children* (2005). As we have seen, in *Final Fantasy VII*, the Lifestream or spirit energy is the source of all planetary life and may be refined into Mako energy. In the movies, the Lifestream concept is more obscure. Rather than Mako, there is Gaia, "the spirit of the planet." Gaia produces the eight spirits that together make an energy wave or beam that is able to transform and repel the Phantom's alien (and presumably incompatible) life spirit. If the concept of Gaia at work in the

Final Fantasy movies seems familiar, that is because the concept is loosely derived from a concept at work in modern ecological science. In ecology, "the Gaia hypothesis" refers to a conjecture proposed by James Lovelock and Lynn Margulis that suggests that the Earth's biosphere is a self-regulating system that maintains conditions favorable to life. So we'll be asking to what extent the concept of Gaia proposed by Lovelock and Margulis is like the concept proposed in *Final Fantasy*. By examining the conception of Gaia from *Final Fantasy*, we can actually sharpen and clarify our understanding of the concept of Gaia at work in the biological and ecological sciences.

AVALANCHE vs. Shinra

In the opening of the movie *Advent's Children*, Marlene Wallace (the daughter of AVALANCHE ecoterrorist Barret Wallace) tells us, "The Lifestream. That's what we call the river of life that circles our planet giving life to the world and everything in it. The Shinra Electric Power Company discovered a way to use the Lifestream as an energy source. Because of Shinra's energy, we were able to live very comfortable lives. Wasn't that because we were taking away from the planet's life? A lot of people thought so."

We might understand what Marlene means by the Lifestream, literally or figuratively. If Marlene is being literal, she is giving a factual report about the actual properties and features of the Lifestream. If she is being figurative, then she is giving a merely metaphorical report—her description will be somewhat like the Lifestream but not exactly like it. The distinction between the literal and the metaphorical matters here because each leads to a very different conception of the Lifestream based on what Marlene is telling us.

If Marlene is simply giving a factual report, then the Lifestream is a very strange thing indeed. The Lifestream is an actual river that circles the planet, giving life to everything, and the planet itself is a living thing that is being killed because the Lifestream is being extracted. It is important to see that if Marlene's description is literal, then the planet, or the world, is a living thing, and presumably by this she means the planet is alive as you are alive or a frog is alive. By offering this description, Marlene would be proposing a conception of the Lifestream that is either *holist* or *organicist*.

Holism is the position that wholes are independent of, or above and beyond, the parts that make them up. If Marlene is giving a holist description of the Lifestream, then she is trying to say that the Lifestream is something more than the rocks, the trees, the critters, the planet, and the energy that make it up. *Organicism* is a position akin to, but subtly and importantly different from, holism. Organicism is the claim that parts cannot exist independently of a whole, just as a heart or a kidney cannot exist as a functioning organ without being part of a larger organism. If this is what Marlene is trying to say, then she would be claiming that fungi, trees, critters, and the planet can exist only insofar as they are part of a larger whole—in this case, the Lifestream.

But what if Marlene is not giving a factual report and is instead giving a metaphorical account of the Lifestream? If Marlene is being metaphorical, the Lifestream is not exactly as she describes it, only somewhat like her description. In metaphorical descriptions, there is always considerable room to maneuver between the description offered and the way things actually are in the world. So, if Marlene's description is metaphorical, not literal, we are free to *interpret* what she says. Once we allow ourselves the latitude to interpret what Marlene says metaphorically, we need not think of the Lifestream in either holist or organicist terms. For example, from Marlene's description, we might understand the Lifestream like this. The Lifestream is the name given to the total, aggregate energy of the planet's environment. This energy "circles" the planet only insofar as everything on the planet is ultimately energy.

Everything on the planet is energy because we know from physics that all matter is simply one form of energy. The Lifestream may be described as "giving life" to everything because anything born on the planet simply takes up materials and energy from the planet. Shinra's artificial extraction of energy is killing the planet, only because nonrenewable energy is being extracted, depleting the available planetary resources and causing pollution.

If we were to accept this interpretation of Marlene's description of the Lifestream, then the Lifestream is simply, and nothing more than, the total energy in the planetary environment. By offering these claims, Marlene would be proposing either a *reductionist* or a *mechanist* conception of the Lifestream. *Reductionism* claims that the properties of wholes are always among the characteristics or the properties of their parts. This is to say that the whole thing has no property that is not a property of at least one of its parts. In other words, the Lifestream has no properties that aren't properties of the planet and the things on the planet. The Lifestream is living only because it is made up of some parts that are living things. *Mechanism* offers the similar claim that the properties of wholes are caused by the parts that make them up. In this view, the parts of the Lifestream cause the whole Lifestream to be alive, even if none of the parts themselves are alive.[1]

Marlene's description of the Lifestream suggests that it may be one of two very different kinds of things. On the one hand, there is the holist-organicist conception of the Lifestream: the Lifestream is a unified whole that has distinct, unique properties not possessed by the rocks, the trees, dirt, and other bits that make it up. The Lifestream as a whole has properties not possessed by any of its parts. On the other hand, there is the reductionist-mechanist conception of the Lifestream, in which the Lifestream is nothing more than an assembly of the rocks, the trees, dirt, and other bits that make it up. All the properties of the Lifestream are simply properties of the stuff that makes up the Lifestream; the Lifestream has no additional special or unique properties of its own.

Deciding between these two conceptions of the Lifestream may seem inconsequential, but underlying the decision is a significant choice between two different and incompatible ways of thinking about the natural world. The conflict between AVALANCHE and Shinra is in part a conflict between these two incompatible views. On the one hand, there is the holist conception of the Lifestream held by the members of AVALANCHE. Tifa Lockheart, Barret Wallace, and the other members of AVALANCHE conceive of the Lifestream as a living whole from which all of the living parts of the world derive their life. On the other hand, there is the mechanist conception of the Lifestream held by the employees of the Shinra Corporation, notably Professor Hojo and Scarlet. Much of the work of Shinra involves taking the Mako extracted from the Lifestream and using it as a simple, interchangeable part for various experiments and projects. Professor Hojo experiments with combining Mako with Jenova cells, while Scarlet oversees the creation of Mako weapons. The incompatibility of holist and mechanist conceptions of the Lifestream ultimately brings AVALANCHE into violent conflict with Shinra.

Dr. Cid, Meet Dr. Lovelock

Although the movie *The Spirits Within* has only a family resemblance with the game *Final Fantasy VII*, it also made use of the Lifestream concept. (This may be because Hironobu Sakaguchi and Kazushige Nojima wrote the scripts for both the game and the movie.) In *The Spirits Within*, the concept of the Lifestream becomes much more obscure. No longer is it possible to interpret the Lifestream as a metaphor for the flow of physical energy. Rather than a Lifestream that is composed of Mako, there is now a Lifestream that is Gaia, "the spirit of the planet." About halfway through the movie, Dr. Cid prompts Aki to read a passage from his old research diary:

> Dr. Aki Ross: [Reading Cid's journal] "All life is born of Gaia, and each life has a spirit. Each new spirit is housed in a physical body." Doctor?
>
> Dr. Cid: Go on.
>
> Dr. Aki Ross: "Through their experiences on Earth, each spirit matures and grows. When the physical body dies, the mature spirit, enriched by its life on Earth, returns to Gaia. Bringing with it the experiences enabling Gaia to live and grow."

Here Dr. Cid is proposing a radical holistic conception of the Lifestream as an organic living creature that lives and grows by imbuing the physical form of things with a living spirit. During its life on the planet, the spirit grows with the accumulation of lived experience, and when it dies, the enlarged spirit returns to Gaia and nourishes it. Thus, the planet, or Gaia, is a single living organism with its own consciousness.

In the 1970s and 1980s, the atmospherologist Dr. James Lovelock and the microbiologist Dr. Lynn Margulis framed what is now called "the Gaia hypothesis." The hypothesis, which was entirely unlike the concept proposed by Dr. Cid, did not suggest that the planet Earth was a living creature, that the Earth has a spirit, or that the Earth is a goddess. Rather, it argued that the Earth's biosphere, including both biota and the physical environment, could be understood as a self-regulating system able to maintain both the climate and the chemical composition of the atmosphere in a state favorable to life. Lovelock defined the Gaia hypothesis as follows: "Gaia is . . . a complex entity involving the Earth's biosphere, atmosphere, oceans, and soil; the totality constituting a feedback or cybernetic system which seeks an optimal physical and chemical environment for life on this planet. The maintenance of relatively constant conditions by active control may be conveniently described by the term homeostasis."[2] In other words, the Gaia hypothesis suggests that there are a number of physical and chemical processes that work together to regulate the chemical content of the biosphere, and through various systems of negative feedback, biospheric conditions favorable for life are maintained.

This view of Gaia is entirely different from Dr. Cid's radical holism. But in what precise way is it different? At first glance, the Gaia hypothesis offered by Lovelock and Margulis appears to be mechanistic. They seem to be arguing that Gaia is made up of physical, chemical, and biological feedback mechanisms. But recall that earlier we defined *mechanism* as the position that the properties of wholes are caused by the parts that make them up. Note that Lovelock and Margulis are *not* simply giving the name Gaia to the combination of mechanisms that regulate environmental conditions. They are making a much larger claim than this! They are claiming that Gaia—the planet Earth—is a *homeostatic* system. Homeostatic systems actively create and maintain stable environments through the interaction of physical and chemical processes. The cells in your body, for example, are parts of a homeostatic system. In your body, each cell releases chemical messengers that give information to other cells about what is needed in order to maintain a stable environment for the efficient functioning of the cell. Other cells respond to that information, while sending out chemical information of their own.

Lovelock argued that the Earth has similar homeostatic properties. He told us that Gaia is "a cybernetic system which seeks an optimal physical and chemical environment for life on this planet." The upshot of this remark is that the mechanisms that make up Gaia are *not* simply causal mechanisms that interact like the parts of a car engine. Rather, Lovelock is claiming that Gaia's mechanisms work together to actively seek or look for optimum environmental conditions for life. That is, on Earth, physical and chemical processes interoperate to maintain and promote the conditions for life on the planet. This is much like saying that the various parts of your car's engine tune themselves automatically for best performance and that the parts of your car repair themselves. The car example highlights the fact that the Gaia concept being proposed by Lovelock is organicist, not purely mechanistic. Recall that organicism is the position that parts cannot exist independently of a whole. Lovelock's Gaia hypothesis is an organicist concept because it suggests that every individual living thing is a part of the whole Earth system and cannot exist apart from that system.

Are the Bad Guys Bad but Right?

In *The Spirits Within*, the hard-nosed General Hein skeptically asks Dr. Cid, "Did you come here to talk about some Gaia theory? To tell us that the planet is alive? That it has a spirit? That's a fairy tale." Hein is right. Dr. Cid does seem to think that the planet has a living spirit, and in the absence of clear evidence, we probably should share General Hein's skepticism. But should we extend that skepticism to the Gaia hypothesis proposed by Lovelock and Margulis? Perhaps not. It isn't clear that the Gaia hypothesis is anything like Dr. Cid's conception of Gaia. Unlike Dr. Cid, Lovelock and Margulis don't suggest either that the Earth has a spirit or that it is alive. They certainly never argue that the Earth has a spirit, and the hypothesis of planetary homeostasis need not commit them to the idea that the Earth is alive. Lovelock and Margulis might remind us that just because living things are good examples of homeostasis, this does not imply that every instance of homeostasis is a living thing.

So despite first appearances, Lovelock and Margulis have a little more in common with Professor Hojo than with

Dr. Cid. I am sure that neither has Hojo's appetite for diabolical schemes and twisted experiments, but like Hojo, Lovelock and Margulis are attempting to understand the physical and chemical processes that maintain planetary homeostasis. Likewise, in his research on Materia, Jenova, and the Cetra, Hojo is attempting to identify underlying physical and chemical causal mechanisms and processes. Admittedly, Hojo does not seem to share Lovelock and Margulis's organicist approach, but, at the same time, neither is engaged in research that proposes anything like Dr. Cid's radical holism. Hojo's approach to science is like that of most real-world scientists. He takes an approach that is mechanistic and reductionistic. Most scientists find reductionism and mechanism attractive because they have been remarkably successful approaches to understanding the natural world.

Yet despite these successes, there have always been philosophers and scientists who have reservations about reductionism and mechanism. In *Final Fantasy VII*, we see this reservation expressed in the radical holistic conception of the Lifestream as an actual living thing with a soul. But in the sciences and philosophy, reservations, about reductionism and mechanism are *not* typically expressed with general arguments for the existence of souls or spirits within. It is more common to make the narrow, simpler argument that living processes and cognition are not straightforwardly mechanistic or reducible. That is, to argue that after mechanistic and reductionist explanations are exhausted, there remains something still to explain. For example, in the seventeenth and eighteenth centuries, some argued that living biological processes could not be fully explained by physical or chemical mechanisms. Life, it was argued, could be explained only by appealing to the existence of an immaterial "vital principle" or "animal soul." This argument was accepted, to some degree, even by famous advocates of mechanism such as René Descartes (1596–1650). In his *Treatise of Man* (c. 1637), he claimed that the physiological functions of man—circulation, digestion, nourishment, and growth—could all be adequately understood as mechanical processes. Yet elsewhere he held that cognitive capacities, such as thinking, judging, and deciding, were not the outcome of mechanical processes but were properties possessed only by human minds.

The problem with arguments that appeal to vital principles, souls, and Lifestreams is that they have been so often defeated. Dr. Cid may seem convincing when he says that there is a vital, living Gaia that is above and beyond physical and chemical principles. But when concepts like this have been proposed and examined empirically, they usually have been found lacking. The ongoing success of mechanism and reductionism, and the ongoing failure to show that there is anything unique or distinctive about living processes, has made most modern scientists suspicious of theories that appeal to anything except reductionist and mechanistic concepts. This suggests that we have good reasons to be suspicious of theories that appeal to holistic concepts. The account of Gaia developed in *The Spirits Within* and *Advent's Children* clearly relies on a dubious holistic concept of the Lifestream. So, General Hein is right to be skeptical of Dr. Cid's theories, and Professor Hojo has some justification (methodological, if not moral) to be pursuing explanations that rely on mechanism and reductionism. But should our skepticism extend to theories that appeal to organicist concepts? Lovelock and Margulis's account of Gaia proposes that living organisms interact to maintain environmental conditions favorable to life through a system of interlocking physical and chemical feedback mechanisms. Should we also be suspicious of the Gaia hypothesis?

The fact that Lovelock and Margulis's Gaia hypothesis is an organicist concept and not purely reductionist or mechanistic has made it enormously controversial in the scientific community. Some scientists dispute the efficacy of specific feedback mechanisms that make up the Gaia system. Others argue that the hypothesis is too sweeping and unspecific to be testable. Still others claim that large-scale homeostasis in ecological systems could not be an outcome of evolution by natural selection. Some, all, or none of these criticisms may turn out, in the long run, to be correct. But aside from these specific empirical criticisms of Gaia, it is worth making the following philosophical observation. In most scientific disciplines, from physics to genetics, hypotheses and explanations employ only reductionist and mechanistic concepts. Ecology and the environmental sciences are noteworthy exceptions. In these disciplines, one is much more likely to encounter hypotheses, such as the Gaia hypothesis, that invoke organicist concepts.[3]

In the closing, climactic scenes of *The Spirits Within*, General Hein is proved utterly wrong and Dr. Cid's hypothesis that the planet has a living spirit called Gaia is vindicated. Aki, the young beautiful protégée of Dr. Cid, desperately tries to persuade Hein that the earth is not under attack by a phantom alien menace. Aki reveals that the mysterious Phantoms are the "confused, lost, and angry" spirits of an alien planet that became stranded when a meteor fragment from their world hit the Earth. The Phantoms are not an alien aggressor but "the living spirit of an alien's home world." Hein ignores Aki and (repeatedly) fires the Zeus Cannon, with devastating consequences. Will Lovelock and Margulis eventually be proved right, just like Dr. Cid is? The answer to this question is unclear. At present, there is little consensus among practicing environmental and ecological scientists about whether organicist concepts are needed to make effective descriptions of the natural world, or whether organicist concepts can be eliminated in favor of reductionist and mechanistic concepts.[4] In the future, Lovelock and Margulis's organicist conception of Gaia may or may not be vindicated. But will Dr. Cid's holistic conception of Gaia ever have a place in the science of our world? No. As we have seen, it contains too many dubious notions that cannot be reconciled with the reductionist and mechanistic features of science. Dr. Cid's Gaia belongs entirely in the world of *Final Fantasy*.

NOTES

1. For further discussion of the concepts of holism, organicism, mechanism, and reductionism, see David Blitz, *Emergent Evolution: Qualitative Novelty and the Levels of Reality* (Boston: Kluwer, 1992).

2. James E. Lovelock, *Gaia: A New Look at Life on Earth* (Oxford: Oxford University Press, 1979, 1989), p. 11.

3. Important examples include Eugene P. Odum, *Ecology: The Link between the Natural and the Social Sciences*, 2nd ed. (New York: Holt, Rinehart and Winston, 1963, 1975); and Richard Levins and Richard C. Lewontin, "Dialectics and Reductionism in Ecology," in *The Dialectical Biologist* (Cambridge, MA: Harvard University Press, 1985).

4. For more on whether a particular conception of nature really matters to environmental ethics, see chapter 5 in this volume, "Gaia and Environmental Ethics in *The Spirits Within*," by Jason P. Blahuta.

GAIA AND
ENVIRONMENTAL ETHICS
IN *THE SPIRITS WITHIN*

Jason P. Blahuta

The Spirits Within, the first movie born of the *Final Fantasy* video game series, presents a bleak vision of humanity's future. An alien meteor has crashed to Earth, bringing with it Phantoms, an ephemeral ensemble of alien creatures that can kill humans with a single touch. Attempts at fighting the alien invaders have been largely ineffective, and the few human beings who remain are fighting a rearguard action, living in fortified cities, with a shield of bio-etheric energy the only thing standing between them and extinction. Among the survivors, General Hein and Doctors Cid and Aki Ross vie for the ruling council's blessing to pursue very different ways of dealing with the aliens.

The general wants to fire the Zeus Cannon—a high-powered laser that allegedly will kill all of the aliens in their nest, the Leonid Meteor. Aki and Dr. Cid want to fight the aliens with a theoretical weapon that Dr. Cid maintains would mirror the bio-etheric energy of the Phantoms, in effect canceling them out. Dr. Cid's weapon is based on a conception of the world that involves the idea of Gaia—that the world possesses a life force—and thus the weapon must be "Gaia-friendly."[1]

A Tale of Two Gaias

The Spirits Within explores a series of debates that are currently raging in our own reality. Most prominent of these is the so-called Gaia hypothesis, advocated by James Lovelock and Lynn Margulis.[2] The Gaia hypothesis is closely related to the concept of Gaia in *The Spirits Within*, but there is a key difference that has to be noted to avoid confusion. Whereas the Gaia of *The Spirits Within* is a substance, literally "the spirit of the Earth," Lovelock's Gaia is more a metaphor that captures the interconnectedness and self-regulating character of Earth: "I call Gaia a physiological system because it appears to have the unconscious goal of regulating the climate and the chemistry at a comfortable state for life. Its goals are not set points but adjustable for whatever is the current environment and adaptable to whatever forms of life it carries," Lovelock stated.[3] But he was quick to qualify his claim with "do not assume that I am thinking of the Earth as alive in a sentient way, or even alive like an animal or bacterium. I think it is time we enlarged the somewhat dogmatic and limited definition of life."[4]

So unlike the *Final Fantasy* Gaia, Earthly Gaia is not the planet's soul, but its ability to self-regulate its environment such that a variety of life forms can flourish. Beyond this key conceptual difference, though, there are a number of important similarities that allow for the exploration of our own environmental crisis. First, both Gaias are the preconditions for all life on their planets. No Gaia, no life, it's that simple. Second, each Gaia supports a multitude of life forms—biodiversity— and appears to be indifferent to which of them thrives or becomes extinct. Consider the attempt to discern a pattern in the Phantoms made by Ryan and Neil, two soldiers who, along with their commanding officer Captain Gray, have extensive experience with Phantoms. Neil comments that it's like "a crazy Noah's ark. . . . You got your human-sized Phantoms, creepy caterpillary Phantoms, and flying Phantoms, and my favorite the big, fat, giant Phantoms. . . . Why would an invading army bring whales and elephants along?" In contrast, Aki's perspective reveals the truth that the Phantoms aren't an invading army but the ghosts of an alien planet's ecosystem. Third, both Gaias can be harmed by the life forms they make possible. The Leonid Meteor is a shard of the alien planet, which was completely destroyed by an apocalyptic war the aliens waged against one another in their pre-Phantom existence.

The Zeus Cannon: A Hein-ous Idea

> Alien Gaia, Earth Gaia. Doctor, even if I believed
> in such nonsense, the fact remains that the Earth
> is under attack from an aggressor who must be
> destroyed at all costs.
>
> —General Hein

The two major approaches to human interaction with the environment that are dominant in our own society are captured by the views of nature and strategies for dealing with the Phantoms advocated by General Hein and Aki. The general espouses a view that is often criticized as a short-sighted, male conception of nature. Hein views nature at best as a collection of inanimate objects subject to humanity's desires and, at worst, something hostile to the human species that needs to be dominated and made to conform to humanity's will. This conception of nature has been traced back to the roots of the Judeo-Christian tradition in the story of Adam's punishment (in Genesis, it is said that after being kicked out of the Garden of Eden, man is condemned to the toilsome task of winning his sustenance from a soil that on his account has been cursed with barrenness) and has been encouraged by philosophers such as Francis Bacon (1561–1626) and René Descartes (1596–1650). Underlying this view of nature is an analytic approach that views aspects of nature in isolation from one another and an assumption that nature is not alive in a meaningful way. It's no surprise that General Hein assumes the Phantoms are an invading army; it's merely an extension of his anthropocentric and militarily trained mind-set.

Aki, by contrast, is representative of both the Gaia hypothesis and some forms of ecofeminism. She views nature not in isolated snapshots that by definition are taken out of context, but holistically and in the context of their dynamic processes.[5] Thus, she echoes the Gaia hypothesis and many contemporary environmentalists in her claims that the planet is, in some sense, alive. Not surprisingly, Aki believes that the best approach to ridding humanity of the Phantoms is to make peace with them, not hit them with things.

General Hein's approach to the Phantoms is doubly flawed. In his quest to persuade the council to give him permission to fire the Zeus Cannon, he creates a breach in the bio-etheric field that protects what is left of New York. The strategy is simple: create a manageable crisis in order to convince the council how dangerous the situation really is. Unfortunately, his lack of understanding of the Phantoms, as well as his arrogance regarding his own intelligence and technological abilities, becomes apparent when the Phantoms travel through the pipes containing bio-etheric energy, something no living entity can do. Unprepared for such a possibility, General Hein watches as his troops are slaughtered, the barrier control station is destroyed, and the city becomes a Phantom playground when the bio-etheric field collapses.

"What have I done?" Hein laments. And for a moment, he seems truly remorseful, because after fleeing from the chaos he created, he contemplates suicide. But for Hein, suicide is not an act of atonement but of self-loathing, and once the possibility of striking at the aliens a second time presents itself, he tries the same stupid strategy again. Hein appeals to the loss of New York to make his case, and the council acquiesces without argument. This time, however, the general's solution is truly heinous—kill the Phantoms by hitting them with the biggest technological stick he can find, the Zeus Cannon.

Hein should know better by this point. Aside from the disaster that he caused in New York, the reasoning was plainly spelled out for him during his initial confrontation with Dr. Cid in front of the council. Dr. Cid told us about what commonly occurs during surgery on patients infected with Phantom particles. The bio-etheric lasers sometimes injure Phantom particles instead of killing them, and these particles just go deeper into the patient's body; when laser power is increased to reach these deeper particles, the patient often incurs further injury and sometimes dies. By analogy, Dr. Cid argues that the Zeus Cannon is likely to have the same effect on a planetary scale. So, while the Zeus Cannon may in fact destroy all of the Phantoms in the Leonid Meteor, it may also leave many injured Phantoms that will merely burrow deeper into the Earth and cause further damage to the planet.

In case the general is forgetful, Aki reminds him that this approach won't work, and the consequences may be the loss not only of a city, but of the entire planet. "Firing on the alien Gaia will only make it stronger," she warns Hein. But the general dismisses her reasoning, blindly committed to his own conception of nature and unwilling to entertain any other ideas. After hitting the Phantoms with several blasts from the Zeus Cannon, his own soldiers tell him they cannot be "sure if it's having any effect." Still, Hein refuses to consider other options and gives the order to fire again. Ultimately, General Hein does get to kill something—himself and all of his soldiers, when he overloads the Zeus Cannon with repeated firings.

The Spirits Within nicely depicts what happens when we disrespect Gaia.[6] Life has a tendency to adapt, and Gaia has a tendency to self-regulate. So when humans meddle extensively with the natural environment, it is not surprising that the nonhuman world adapts to our interventions and, as it were, strikes back. Failure to acknowledge this results from the myopic attitude of General Hein, who insists the problem is mechanical in nature: alien creatures come from the Meteor Crater, so he should attack the crater with the Zeus Cannon. Ironically, Newtonian laws of physics (which are purely mechanistic) call for reactions. So people like General Hein, who think they can interfere with the workings of a complex machine without instigating some form of reaction, possess a very shallow understanding of the machine they are playing with. One doesn't have to accept the Gaia hypothesis to realize that intervention invites blowback.

Aki's approach to the Phantoms is very different. Dr. Cid's bio-etheric wave is a Gaia-friendly weapon that will cancel the Phantoms out, but Aki's language sheds light on a very different strategy from Hein's. In her last reasoned plea to the general, she argues that the Phantoms are ghosts, "spirits that are confused, lost, and angry." The solution that she and Dr. Cid offer is not so much about killing them as it is putting them to rest. Spiritual imagery aside, the point is clear: her strategy for dealing with environmental problems involves a sense of equilibrium with other entities in the environment. In the case of the Phantoms, this means understanding them and what they need. As suffering ghosts, they need to rest. The bio-etheric wave will allow them to do this, whereas the Zeus Cannon will not.

Aki represents open-mindedness to nature. When the first blast of the Zeus Cannon kills the eighth spirit, Captain Gray, Dr. Cid, and Aki all lose hope. The eighth spirit was necessary to complete the energy wave, and if the spirit has been killed, then there is no way to stop the Phantoms. But while Dr. Cid despairs and Gray resorts to tactical thinking in an utterly hopeless situation, Aki manages to complete the energy wave. She succeeds not by aggressively looking for the eighth spirit or by trying to find a technological fix for the weapon's incompleteness, but by simply being open to it. In the end, the final spirit finds Aki; all she has to do is be open to recognizing its presence.

Gaia's Revenge and the Fate of Humanity

> Doctor, there is a war going on. No one's young anymore.
>
> —Aki

The major monotheistic religions of the West have highly anthropocentric worldviews, greatly privileging humanity. The entire universe (and not merely the tiny speck of it called Earth) was supposedly created for humans, and our species is allegedly superior to all others, therefore playing a commanding role in the world. Humanity isn't simply the reason for creation, it is creation's temporal master. The Gaia hypothesis threatens this puffed-up self-importance in a radical way. Not only are we not the reason for the Earth's existence, but we are no more special than any other species on the planet. The Gaia hypothesis maintains that humans (and not only lawyers and politicians) have no more moral worth than does any other member of the biotic community, maggots included.

Environmentalists generally aren't suggesting that we should drastically change our lives to accommodate maggots. With the possible exception of the most radical of their group, environmentalists still privilege the human species above all other species whenever conflicts of interest pop up between humanity and other species. Environmentalists, however, do protest the nature of these conflicts of interest and how they are adjudicated. Traditionally, nonhuman entities—be they animals, plants, or even entire ecosystems—lose whenever a conflict with human interests arises. Environmentalists of all stripes have been insisting for decades that this practice has to change, that we need to understand the nonhuman world in a way that acknowledges its value. Once the nonhuman world has value, then it is possible for it to stand its ground when human interests want to impinge on it.

The question, though, is how do we assess the value of the nonhuman world? Environmentalist approaches to value and the natural world fall into two broad categories. The first argues that nature possesses intrinsic or inherent worth (that is to say, an animal has value in and of itself, regardless of what use it has to humans or other species). So any use of the planet or other life forms that is based in self-interest is anthropocentric (human centered) and unethical. The second category is unconcerned with why we value something, so long as we do value it. What matters, people on this side will argue, are the consequences of our actions. It is irrelevant whether we refrain from buying shampoos tested on baby bunny rabbits because we respect nature, merely find baby bunnies cute, or somehow see the fate of humanity tied to a biodiversity that includes baby bunnies—all that matters is that we don't buy the bunny-tested shampoo. For this group, if anthropocentrism and enlightened, long-term self-interest lead to the same environmentally friendly practices that viewing nature as intrinsically valuable do, why get side tracked about the details?

The Gaia hypothesis does more than merely dethrone humanity, reducing us to one species on an even footing with all of the others. Ozone depletion, soil and water degradation, increased levels of greenhouse gasses, loss of biodiversity—all fueled by an expanding population with ever increasing dreams of living in material affluence—have transformed humanity from being merely one species among many into a cancer that is slowly eating away at the regenerative processes of the planet.[7]

This view of humanity fits well with the portrayal of people in *The Spirits Within*. Lovelock argued that if humanity keeps on behaving the way it presently is, within a few decades we will (and may already) have inflicted sufficient damage on Gaia's ability to self-regulate that her "revenge" (a misleading term, because even if alive, Gaia is completely indifferent to all species, humanity included) will be felt as her regenerative processes fail. Global warming will play havoc with weather systems, loss of ozone will kill off massive amounts of animal and plant life that don't have time to adapt to radically increased ultraviolet radiation, and fresh drinkable water, already in short supply throughout much of the world, will become increasingly scarce. The result, according to Lovelock, is that humanity will likely be reduced from its present state of grandeur to one of huddled groups of survivors, mostly located in polar regions, violently clashing over the few remaining food sources available, waiting and hoping that some day in the distant future Gaia will recover so that the Earth's environment will become amenable to human society again.

Who Cares?

You've been trying to tell me that death isn't the end.

—Captain Gray

Thomas Malthus (1766–1834), an English political economist most famous for his *Essay on the Principle of Population*, postulated a self-regulating correlation between food supply and population levels. From a Malthusian perspective we've pushed the envelope as far as it can go, and a mighty "Malthus check" lies in wait for us. Billions will die of all sorts of plagues, diseases, and wars over resources, until the human population's size is in an appropriate relationship to the food supply. Malthus was speaking strictly about discrepancies between food supply and population, but he can be adapted to the

Gaia hypothesis quite easily. The Earth has an immense but limited ability to act as the source of all of our activities and as a sink for all of the wastes and by-products of these activities. But once the human population's size becomes large enough that its activities overwhelm this ability of the Earth to act as a source and a sink, the system will begin to break down. Gaia will, temporarily at least, be unable to self-regulate. The consequences will be massive loss of life forms, which means less food and, if not human extinction, at least a culling of the human population. The only really important question, from a Gaia hypothesis standpoint, is, will Gaia survive? Will humanity go into remission, or are we a terminal cancer that will permanently destroy Gaia's functioning?

But why should we care? Admittedly, the loss of human civilization is disappointing to most humans, but two things need to be considered before we get all weepy about our bleak future. First, we are not necessary to Gaia. Furthermore, if Lovelock is right, our behavior is sufficiently harmful to Gaia and our willingness to change so minimal that Gaia would be better off without us. Second, in the long run Gaia is doomed anyway. Gaia and all of life that she makes possible will die in about five billion years when the sun dies, and that's assuming her ability to self-regulate is not destroyed first by a gamma ray burst from a nearby star going supernova or maimed by a massive meteor impact.

A Cancerous Tumor Inside Gaia

So if the Gaia hypothesis or *The Spirits Within* teaches us anything, it's how interconnected the natural world is and how unnecessary we are. Far from being the lords and masters of nature, human societies have become, at best, tyrants—and at worst, cancerous. If we want our role to continue, whether for anthropocentric or nonanthropocentric reasons, we need to ensure that our interactions with nature become less damaging.

There are only two ways to do that: either control our lifestyles so that we do not overwhelm the Earth's ability to act as a source and a sink, or control our population to the same effect. Either way, humanity is little more than a cancerous tumor inside Gaia, and the fate of the species depends on whether we choose to be a benign or a malignant tumor.

NOTES

1. For more on the Gaia hypothesis, see chapter 4 in this volume: "The Lifestream, Mako and Gaia," by Jay Foster.

2. The Gaia hypothesis has gone through a number of articulations over the years. I will refer to Lovelock's most recent version of it, *The Revenge of Gaia: Earth's Climate Crisis and the Fate of Humanity* (New York: Basic Books, 2006).

3. Ibid., p. 15.

4. Ibid., p. 16.

5. See Carolyn Merchant, *The Death of Nature: Women, Ecology and the Scientific Revolution* (New York: HarperCollins, 1989) for a detailed account of the enlightenment approach to nature, as well as the response of some feminist scholars.

6. The idea that alien Gaias exist is not all that far-fetched, if Gaia is merely a conceptual image to express the complexities of an integrated, self-regulating system conducive to certain forms of life (not unlike a human body). Some scientists have estimated that there are as many as half a million such planets in the Milky Way galaxy alone. See Siegfried Franck, Werner von Bloh, Christine Bounama, and Hans-Joachim Schellnhuber, "Extraterrestrial Gaias," in Stephen H. Schneider, James R. Miller, Eileen Crist, and Penelope J. Boston, eds., *Scientists Debate Gaia: The Next Century* (Cambridge, MA: MIT Press, 2004), pp. 309–319.

7. Lovelock disagreed, claiming, "Humans are not merely a disease; we are, through our intelligence and communication, the nervous system of the planet," p. xiv. He never provides any substantive argument, however, as to why the human species is at all valuable from a perspective other than that of the human species.

OBJECTIFICATION OF CONSCIOUS LIFE FORMS IN *FINAL FANTASY*

Robert Arp and Sarah Fisk

Use Me, Even in Your Fantasies . . .

The *Final Fantasy* franchise is rife with examples of immorality. For example, in the most recent *Final Fantasy* movie, *Advent Children*, a trio of maliciously minded brothers kidnaps children afflicted with a disease known as *Geostigma*, in an attempt to use them to revive Jenova. As you know, Jenova is an evil extra-terrestrial life form, first introduced in the game *Final Fantasy VII*, which is capable of being used for mass destruction whenever its cells are brought out of dormancy and spread. The cells can carry out Jenova's will using its power even when they are separated from the whole being. The trio of brothers intends to use the children to aid in bringing Jenova back to life. In the story the children are objectified, treated as if they were objects—treated simply as a means to an end, nothing more. Although we are clearly meant to interpret the brothers' actions as immoral, can ethical theory support this interpretation?

Three Reasons *Not to Use* Life Forms . . . and Three Reasons *to Use* Life Forms

Throughout the history of Western philosophy, we find three prominent moral theories, each of which can help us understand the ethics of objectification. First, there is the view originated by Immanuel Kant (1724–1804) that persons, by virtue of their conscious rational capacities, are free and autonomous beings, possessing inalienable worth and dignity. Because of this intrinsic worth, a person should *never* be treated as a mere object. Consider *Final Fantasy IX*. In this game, the arms dealer Kuja blatantly uses Queen Brahne as a puppet to accomplish his own goals of achieving a kind of ultimate power. Queen Brahne behaves erratically throughout the game until it is revealed that Kuja is manipulating her. When she tries to rebel, Kuja kills her and destroys her army.

A second moral theory is the utilitarian view of John Stuart Mill (1806–1873), which asserts that actions are morally good insofar as they maximize the aggregate happiness of all people. That is, an action is good insofar as it brings about the greatest happiness for the greatest number of people. Specifically, Mill is concerned with pleasure as being of ultimate importance and thus with maximizing pleasure and minimizing pain. In this view, rampant objectification is immoral because suffering and unhappiness typically thrive where people are worried that they will be exploited in their social interactions.

Final Fantasy IX features much manipulation and exploitation. As previously mentioned, it is discovered that Kuja, the arms dealer, has been manipulating Queen Brahne of Alexandria in the hopes of gaining ultimate power. Toward the end of the game, it is further revealed that the events in this world have been planned and executed to further the goal of transforming the dying world, Terra, into another world, Gaia. All of the events and the characters in the game have been carefully manipulated to bring about this transformation. To assist in the transformation, the people of Terra created Garland, a powerful old man. All of the people of Gaia were created by the powerful Garland to house the souls of the people of Terra once the transformation of worlds was complete. All parties are angry with this, including Kuja, who discovers that he is merely a defective precursor to another, more important, character. Kuja responds to this by destroying Terra.

A third moral theory is the virtue ethics view, held by Aristotle (384–322 BCE). Virtue ethics sees morally right actions as stemming from virtuous characters. Here, objectification can be considered immoral because it originates from, as well as reinforces, a nonvirtuous (vicious) character. Professor Hojo, a character in *Final Fantasy VII*, fits Aristotle's conception of a vicious character. In his experimentation on sentient beings in an attempt to combine them with extraterrestrial life forms, Hojo is responsible for the creation of Sephiroth, another destructive character. Clearly, Hojo acts without regard for ethical considerations, such as the effect of his actions or the nature of those actions. Such despicable behavior is exactly what a virtue ethicist would expect from someone having a weak or wicked character.

There *are* times, however, when each of these three theories can be interpreted broadly to suggest that someone actually has done the right thing in objectifying another person. First, a Kantian might argue that it's morally acceptable for a person—by virtue of being a rational, autonomous agent—to give permission to be used by others. In *Final Fantasy VIII*, the main character, Squall, learns that a girl named Ellone is sending him back in time. She does all of this in order to attempt to change the events of the past. Squall willingly allows this to happen—knowing full well that he might get hurt or die—and the important point is that Squall is a rational agent who takes charge of his own destiny in allowing this to take place.

Second, a utilitarian would argue that it's morally acceptable to sacrifice a member of a group in order to save the rest of its members. Each of the three playable characters of *Final Fantasy X-2* can acquire the ability to sacrifice his or her life to damage an enemy severely during active battle. This means that this character dies and does not collect any experience, but if the battle is successfully completed, the character may be able to damage the enemy sufficiently to allow other characters to defeat the enemy and then bring the fallen character back to life.

Third, a virtue ethicist (though not Aristotle) might argue that self-preservation and power are the highest virtues and might justify retaining them by *any* means. Seifer, one of the antagonists of *Final Fantasy VIII*, embodies this very notion. He becomes dissatisfied with doing his assigned duty of carrying out the Garden's orders and figures that it is better to have autonomy over his own actions and decide for himself who he will work for.[1] Seifer believes that he should be the leader of the groups with whom he works, and he determines that leaving the group on his own will lead to both self-preservation and power. Seifer's character clearly values his own existence as extremely important and also values the accumulation of power as valuable in itself.

Kant vs. Shinra

The *Final Fantasy* series is rich in illustrations of moral "stalemates" or inconsistencies for the Kantian and utilitarian systems, similar to the ones already mentioned. These stalemates call the legitimacy of the two approaches into question concerning their attitudes toward objectification. This leaves an Aristotelian version of virtue ethics as the most viable of the three major moral perspectives, if for the primary reason that it does not clearly generate such stalemates.

Kant grounded morality in the fact that persons are rational beings. Since it is only by reason that we determine and perform our moral obligations, rational will is the only thing that is unconditionally good.[2] By virtue of the fact that all people possess rationality, they are worthy of dignity and respect and are the only things that are "ends in themselves." Given that people are entirely precious in this way, they always have *intrinsic* value (as ends) and must never be treated as having merely *instrumental* value (as a means to an end), like some instrument. So, it would be immoral for one person to use another exclusively as a means to further some end, goal, or purpose because, by doing so, the used person would be reduced to the status of a lowly tool.[3]

This intrinsic value could be extended to other rationally conscious beings from other worlds, even though they are made up of different substances such as alternate brain mass (elves), plasma (aliens), or silicon and metal (robotic mechanisms). For example, in *Final Fantasy VII*, an evil corporation, known as Shinra, is draining the life force of the very planet itself. The planet is viewed as a sentient being, whose energy comes from what is known as the Lifestream. The Lifestream is composed of the essences that power the physical bodies of the inhabitants of the planet for each inhabitant's life span. When the planet's inhabitants die, their essences are returned to the Lifestream.

Given that persons are conscious, rational beings, capable of making their own free and informed decisions, Kant demanded that they must also be respected in virtue of being *autonomous* ("self-ruling") beings. Now, because a person's innate dignity and worth are tied to rational autonomy, some post-Kantian thinkers have argued that what is most significant in making a moral decision has to do with whether a person's *freedom in rationally informed decision-making* has been respected.[4]

The idea here is that if a fully rational person chooses to engage in some action—as long as the action doesn't harm anyone else—then that person is fully justified in doing it, even if it puts him or her in the position of being used like an object. Think of rational adults joining the military knowing that they may die protecting their country. Similarly, as long as the various henchmen of villains know full well the risks that they are assuming by aiding and abetting criminals, then there is nothing immoral in the villains treating the henchmen as if they are dispensable (but this is not to say that any of the other actions of the villains or the henchmen are morally acceptable). In other words, as long as these rational agents all freely agree to engage in such behaviors, then there is nothing morally wrong in objectifying them.

The experience of summoning Guardian Forces (GFs) in *Final Fantasy VIII* can help illustrate this point. Members of the players' party can summon various Guardian Forces that overtake their bodies and transform them, all for the purpose of defeating the enemy with a greater show of power. These Guardian Forces must be discovered within the game, and often a player must defeat them in battle before the GFs will agree to assist the player.

But how can we decide whether we should ever use people as mere instruments? Don't fully rational persons have the freedom to make their own well-informed decisions? There is one camp of "moral sanctity" Kantians who would argue that it's immoral to objectify a person, no matter what.[5] But there is another group of "moral autonomy" Kantians who would contend that as long as all parties are fully aware of the risks of the situation, nothing immoral occurs in consensual objectification. As long as the party members are well aware that they can be killed when they are transformed by a GF and that they lose the ability to control their bodies, then nothing immoral is taking place. In fact, "moral autonomy" Kantians often argue that to deny a person the freedom to so choose would itself be immoral because such a denial violates a person's autonomy as a rational, free decision maker. In other words, refusing to allow people to make their own choices is to reduce them to objects, because, after all, mere objects lack choices.[6] Based on Kant's philosophy, however, neither can be more important than the other—both are indispensable.

A Utilitarian Moral Stalemate: Sacrificing Party Members

Although most utilitarians would admit that both sanctity and autonomy are important, the foundation of morality, as far as they're concerned, is simply happiness—actions are good insofar as they increase the pleasures or decrease the pains of people, in general.[7] The reason this view is termed *utilitarian* is that the true test of an action's propriety is whether it has useful consequences (utility) with respect to promoting happiness. In opposition to the strict Kantian view that persons never should be used merely as means to some end, the utilitarian position has no problem treating some people as means, if, as a result, the "sum total" of happiness is increased for all people.[8]

The *Final Fantasy* series abounds with examples of actions justified by utilitarian-type reasons. The female character Yuna, of *Final Fantasy X* and *X-2*, is in fact best characterized by her sacrificial actions as Summoner for the people of her world, Spira. At the conclusion of *Final Fantasy X*, her love interest, Tidus, disappears due to the status of his physical being. We discover, in *Final Fantasy X-2*, that rather than pursue Tidus or try to bring him back, Yuna has gone back to her home in Besaid to serve her people. She is finally convinced to pursue him when she feels as though her people can carry on successfully without her constant supervision. Most of Yuna's decisions in the game revolve around doing what is best for her people and for the planet, not what is in her own best interests.

Her decisions clearly follow a pattern of doing the greatest good for the majority of her people.

Another example of this formula for ethical decision making can be found in *Final Fantasy VII*. In this game, one of the main characters, Aeris, sacrifices her own well-being and ultimately her own life trying to defeat an enemy that is destroying the planet. Although Aeris is killed by the embodiment of the enemy, Sephiroth, she sacrifices her life attempting to defend not only the planet itself, but all of its inhabitants.

Finally, the conflict between Kantianism and utilitarianism is never clearer than when young graduates from the various training Gardens of *Final Fantasy VIII* are assigned to foreign armies or governments. The graduates themselves have no choice in the matter. As we see in the development of the game, some of the foreign countries turn on their neighbors and begin to attack them, thus putting the entire planet in peril. It is the duty of the graduating soldiers to serve the army or the government to which they are assigned, however, even at the cost of the well-being of everyone else on the planet. When the graduates are given a mission, they are often unaware of the possible consequences of the mission. They simply carry out their orders as per their duty to serve those to whom they have been assigned.

We have already noted that Kant's theory presented us with a moral stalemate because it implied that objectification is *both* good and bad in some scenarios. Another kind of stalemate arises from the utilitarian perspective. A strict utilitarian must admit that an action is good, no matter how horribly some people are treated, so long as more people benefit in the long run.[9] This means that if killing certain people will increase the overall happiness of humanity, then such murder is not only permissible but downright advisable, based on utilitarianism. For example, imagine the risks to innocent bystanders in various games when your party fights monsters or major antagonists. There is always the risk that these people may be injured in the fighting, but the overall happiness of humanity depends on your defeat of the aggressors. Furthermore, if some of your party members die in the attempt to save the world you are defending, this is all part and parcel of the mission you have been entrusted with. More often than not, in the worlds of *Final Fantasy*, this mission involves the well-being of many, sometimes entire worlds. The fate of everyone and everything in a world often depends on your success and if your success means the end of your life, then you are expected to give it. Thus, a utilitarian regards such self-sacrifice as obligatory, and if you decline to give up your life, other people are justified in taking it.

Maybe a few utilitarians could bite the bullet and claim that this conclusion is acceptable, but most of them would admit that it is too extreme.[10] Although mandatory self-sacrifice would create a tremendous amount of happiness for some people, the amount of misery for the widows, the families, and the friends of the departed would be just as substantial. Such a system would induce paranoia, undermine security, and destroy humanity as we know it, thereby making it worse. Indeed, you can imagine this state of affairs culminating in a single living person, so pleased with his solitude that killing everyone else was warranted. Such an outcome is not merely tragicomic, it is absurd. A utilitarian stalemate, then, results from the fact that by holding the greatest happiness of the greatest number in such high regard, it *unacceptably* advocates decreasing the latter number as a means of increasing the former balance.

Virtue Ethics: Aristotle, Aeris, and Sephiroth

Opposed to these *action-based* moral theories, which first establish what people should do and then assess whether they have actually done so, there are *character-based* theories, which first look at how people actually act and *then* determine how they should act.[11]

Aristotle, in particular, thought that character development was the key to morality. As he saw it, our characters result from our (1) forming certain habits starting in childhood and (2) acquiring practical wisdom in maturity. Ideally, people would cultivate the habits and form the wisdom that would lead them to know how to always act in the right way, at the right time, in the right manner, and for the right reasons. He famously believed that the path of such uprightness always ends up being the mean between two extremes. For example, courageous people are neither cowardly nor reckless, but somewhere in between.

An example of a plainly virtuous character is Aeris of *Final Fantasy VII*, who embodies virtues of liberality and courage. Aeris risks her life to help save the planet and its people. An example of a plainly vicious character is Sephiroth, who is malicious and viciously ambitious. His ultimate goal in the game is the destruction of the planet—mainly out of spite.

Friedrich Nietzsche (1844–1900) advocated a form of virtue ethics that was very different from that of Aristotle. Nietzsche believed that power was the ultimate virtue, and that we all must express power *if we are powerful.*[12] Society consists of domineering master–slave relationships. Some people have the kind of character that causes them to be attracted to being in control; others are prone to being controlled. For example, the character of Cloud in *Final Fantasy VIII* is attracted to being in control, whereas his nemesis, Seifer, is prone to being controlled. Cloud enjoys dictating his own destiny, and sometimes this brings him into conflict with authorities. Seifer, on the other hand, seeks power at any cost, even allowing himself to be controlled by a sorceress in an attempt to secure power for himself.[13]

So, What Character Do You Aspire to Be?

Can virtue ethics tell us if and when objectification is warranted without falling into the same stalemate traps that the Kantian and utilitarian positions did? Aristotle escaped the problems that Kant faced because even if we suppose that sanctity and autonomy are equally important, a person who encroaches on either would simply show that he or she has a weak character. A virtuous, well-balanced person tends not to objectify people because objectification is an extreme action. On rare occasions, however, objectification can be the right course of action. For example, when people courageously (as opposed to rashly) allow themselves to be used by others, they are demonstrating their own virtuous characters, such as the case of Aeris. Thus, for Aristotle, the conflict between sanctity and autonomy is illusory—one of the two is always the right target. Because Aristotle would have said that only vicious people achieve happiness at other people's expense, the difficulty that plagued utilitarianism also does not apply.

Nietzsche simply advocated living your life to the fullness of your potential. If your greatest attribute is intelligence, do not feign stupidity to appease the masses. Similarly, if you're camera shy, don't try to become a movie star. Rather, just be yourself! Don't let anyone tell you what you should believe or that sanctity is a virtue. It is, in fact, a vice that is meant to make you live like everyone else. Instead, determine for yourself what to believe, and you will experience a joyful wisdom that most people aren't even capable of. Simply put, always express your autonomy, and you will never act "wrongly." Nietzsche did not encounter the Kantian stalemate because, for him, autonomy is clearly more important than sanctity. He also sidestepped the utilitarian problem because he was not concerned with happiness at all. Utilitarians mistakenly think all men are created equal and deserve equal treatment—this is the source of their stalemate.

Aeris or a Cloud?

The two virtue ethics perspectives we've considered don't have the problems that plagued the moral theories of Kant and Mills. But which virtue ethics perspective is the better one to uphold and foster in one's life? In other words, which kind of person should we strive to be, Aristotle's eudaimon (virtuous man) or Nietzsche's Übermensch (superman)? More to the point, whom do *you* most aspire to be: an Aeris or a Cloud? Ultimately, the decision is yours.

NOTES

1. The various Gardens are places where young people train to become mercenaries and members of a militarylike organization that takes on special missions and jobs. Often the jobs are dangerous and involve putting down rebellions or defeating evil characters. The role of the graduates, or SeeD members, is to potentially risk their lives to accomplish the mission or protect the team. Following orders in such a group is of utmost importance.

2. Rational will is the expression of our free will by our acting in accordance with rationality instead of irrationality and sensuality.

3. See Immanuel Kant, *Foundations of the Metaphysics of Morals*, translated by Lewis White Beck (Upper Saddle River, NJ: Prentice Hall, 1989). See also Onora O'Neill, *Constructions of Reason: Explorations of Kant's Practical Philosophy* (Cambridge, UK: Cambridge University Press, 1990).

4. See Thomas Hill, *Autonomy and Self-Respect* (New York: Cambridge University Press, 1991); Christine Korsgaard, *The Sources of Normativity* (New York: Cambridge University Press, 1996); and Timothy Madigan, "The Discarded Lemon: Kant, Prostitution and Respect for Persons," *Philosophy Now* 21 (1998): 14–16.

5. See Andrea Dworkin, *Pornography: Men Possessing Women* (New York: Perigee Press, 1981); and Catherine MacKinnon, *Feminism Unmodified: Discourses on Life and Law* (Cambridge, MA: Harvard University Press, 1988).

6. See Ann Garry, "Pornography and Respect for Women," in John Arthur, ed., *Morality and Moral Controversies* (Upper Saddle River, NJ: Prentice-Hall, 1993), pp. 395–421; Timothy Madigan, "The Discarded Lemon: Kant, Prostitution and Respect for Persons," *Philosophy Now* 21 (1998): 14–16; and Sibyl Schwarzenbach, "On Owning the Body," in James Elias, Vern Bullough, Veronica Elias, and Gwen Brewer, eds., *Prostitution: On Whores, Hustlers, and Johns* (New York: Prometheus Books, 1998), pp. 345–351.

7. See, for example, John Stuart Mill, *On Liberty* (New York: Meridian, 1974).

8. See Jeremy Bentham, *An Introduction to the Principles of Morals and Legislation* (Garden City, NY: Doubleday, 1961); John Stuart Mill, *Utilitarianism* (Indianapolis: Hackett Publishing Company, 2002); and Peter Singer, *Practical Ethics* (Cambridge: Cambridge University Press, 1993).

9. Many thinkers have argued that "goods" can result from "evils" to justify the existence of God or the forces of nature in the face of egregious evil. Classical examples are G. W. Leibniz, *Theodicy* (London: Routledge & Kegan Paul Limited, 1996), and Viktor Frankl, *Man's Search for Meaning* (Boston: Beacon Press, 1959). For more

contemporary work, see John Hick, ed., *Dialogues in the Philosophy of Religion* (New York: Macmillan, 2001).

10. See J. J. C. Smart, "An Outline of a System of Utilitarian Ethics," in J. J. C. Smart and Bernard Williams, *Utilitarianism: For and Against* (New York: Cambridge University Press, 1973).

11. The idea here—which was noted by philosophers as far back as Confucius (551–479 BCE) and Plato (c. 427–347 BCE)—is that different people have different characters.

12. Friedrich Nietzsche, *Beyond Good and Evil*, translated by Walter Kaufmann (New York: Random House, 1966), and *The Will to Power*, translated by Walter Kaufmann (New York: Random House, 1967). For contemporary examples of virtue ethics theories employing the concept of power, see Imelda Whelehan, *Modern Feminist Thought: From Second Wave to "Post-Feminism"* (New York: New York University Press, 1995), and Marti Hohmann, "Prostitution and Sex-Positive Feminism," in *Prostitution: On Whores, Hustlers, and Johns*.

13. For discussions of other aspects of Nietzsche's philosophy as it relates to the *Final Fantasy* series, please see chapter 2, "Kefka, Nietzsche, Foucault: Madness and Nihilism in *Final Fantasy VI*," by Kylie Prymus; chapter 11, "Sin, Otherworldliness, and the Downside to Hope," by David Hahn; and chapter 12, "Human, All Too Human: Cloud's Existential Quest for Authenticity," by Christopher R. Wood, all in this volume.

PART THREE

ABILITIES YOU NEVER KNEW YOU HAD

FINAL FANTASY AND THE
PURPOSE OF LIFE

Greg Littmann

Hey, where are you four brats off to now? What . . . ?
You're going to go save the world . . . ? Did you get
hit on the head or something!?

—Woman in Ur, *Final Fantasy III*

The oldest game in the world must be pretending to be someone else. Even before children learn to speak, they start to
copy the adults around them and they soon start to act out
better and more exciting lives, whether it be putting a stop to
crime or exploring new planets. Some people grow out of it as
they get older. Suckers. The rest of us just start playing more
sophisticated games. Thanks to the steady advancement of
computer technology, things have never been better for those
of us who enjoy exploring lives that are not our own, and nothing demonstrates this more clearly than the *Final Fantasy* series
of video games, which has offered new lives to hundreds of
thousands of people since 1987. The phenomenal success
of the *Final Fantasy* series makes it a natural resource for

investigating the question of the purpose, or the best purpose, of life in the real world. After all, role-playing games are only successful if they tempt us with lives that seem worth living.

Of course, just because we enjoy pretending that something is happening doesn't automatically mean that we think it would be good in real life. For example, we might be having fun when a Cactaur impales us with a thousand flying needles in a *Final Fantasy* game, but that doesn't mean we think that suffering a comparable injury in the real world would be a good thing. Similarly, if we are playing *Final Fantasy XI Online*, we might regard it as a little harmless, black-humored fun to run around the Batallia Downs slaughtering the poor little Pixies, but no sane person thinks that killing intelligent creatures just for fun is all right in real life.

The purpose of this chapter is to investigate the question of what kinds of lives we should be living in the real world, by contrasting the "lives" that are held to be well lived in the worlds of *Final Fantasy* with the sorts of lives recommended by philosophers. In particular, we'll look at what the philosophers Thomas Hobbes (1588–1679), John Stuart Mill (1806–1873), and Aristotle (384–322 BCE) would say about the lives lived by the protagonists of the *Final Fantasy* computer games and in particular about the lives chosen by players of *Final Fantasy XI Online*.

Hobbes vs. the Hobgoblins

> Citizens, unite! Come to the light. . . . Real happiness can be found in obedience to the company.
>
> —President Shinra, *Final Fantasy VII*

Hobbes believed that the fundamental moral rule is that people should act in their own self-interest. He thought that you have no moral obligation to help other people unless helping them will benefit you in the long run, and whether you harm someone else is irrelevant except insofar as he or she might harm you back. So, for example, it would be immoral to mug a Tarutaru and take its gils if you are likely to get caught, but mugging the Tarutaru would be the right thing to do if you could get away with it. Philosophers call the view that we should do whatever is in our best interests "moral egoism."

All of this might make Hobbes sound like an anarchist, but in fact, he thought that it was in people's best interests to live in obedience to an absolute monarch. Most monarchists of Hobbes's day believed that a monarch's authority comes from God, but Hobbes maintained that it comes from the monarch's own subjects. The subjects are considered to be partners in a social contract with one another, in which they mutually agree to give up certain freedoms, in the interest of the common good. In particular, they agree to be ruled by a king, on the grounds that only such a powerful central authority can keep order and peace. Because order and peace are in everyone's best interests, it is in everyone's interests to make sure that he or she obeys the king's law and does nothing to undermine the king's authority. After all, where there is no law and no authority, everyone is in danger from everyone else. To take an example from *Final Fantasy*, even a badass like Cloud Strife has to sleep sometime, and when he does, he could be murdered by any weakling unless someone else is watching out for him. Hobbes called this lawless alternative to monarchy "the state of nature" and said that life under it is "solitary, poor, nasty, brutish and short," a "war of every man against every man."[1] Hobbes believed that the very worst form of disobedience to the monarch was to rebel against him or her, because even the worst monarchies are preferable to the horrors that occur during civil war. If Hobbes's philosophy interests you, I recommend his book *Leviathan*.[2]

Hobbes would think that most of the protagonists of the solo *Final Fantasy* games are fools. After all, he thought that our guiding concern in life should be personal self-interest, and if there is one thing the protagonists of the solo *Final Fantasy* games are known for, it is putting aside self-interest. In fact, they tend to devote their lives to the well-being of other people. The very first *Final Fantasy* game focuses on four adventurers striving to return the world's elements to a state of balance, the second on four adventurers striving to save the world from conquest at the hands of the evil dictator Palamecia, the third on four adventurers seeking to return balance again, while the fourth through tenth are respectively about Heroes striving to save the world from the Warrior Golbez, the Wizard Exdeath, the dictator Gestahl, the mastermind Sephiroth, the Sorceress Edea, the warmongering Queen Brahne, and the giant monster Sin. The most recent solo game, *Final Fantasy XII*, is similarly themed. It's about a small group of adventurers standing up against the might of the evil Archadian Empire. The Heroes of *Final Fantasy* are so altruistic that Hobbes would be disgusted at their obsessive dedication to promoting the common good.

You might think that I'm being naive about the motives of the Heroes here. After all, even though the protagonists are out to save the world, the world they are saving is the world they live in, and saving the world you live in is something that is ultimately in every person's self-interest, regardless of how selfish he or she may be. For example, Tidus from *Final Fantasy X* may be striving to rid Spira of the rampaging monster Sin, but Tidus is in just as much danger from Sin's surprise attacks as anyone else on Spira is. At the beginning of the game, Sin has already destroyed Tidus's home city of Zanarkand, and Tidus has every reason to believe that if Sin strikes his location again, he won't get away with his life. Similarly, Cloud Strife from *Final Fantasy VII* might be fighting to prevent the world of Gaia from being enslaved by Shinra corporation and the would-be god Sephiroth, but if Sephiroth were to succeed, Cloud Strife himself would be just as much a slave as anyone else was. In light of this, it could be argued that the characters are very much acting in accordance with their own self-interest and so are acting in a way that Hobbes would approve of.

I don't think Hobbes would buy this argument for a second, though. It might be true that the Heroes are saving their own skins along with everyone else's, but what we know of their characters almost always tells us that they are doing it out of sheer nobility. The four Light Warriors of the very first *Final Fantasy* don't seem to have any purpose in life other than doing good for others, appearing out of nowhere in accordance with prophecy to bring balance to the world. Similarly, the rebel Heroes of *Final Fantasy II* put themselves in great personal danger to overthrow the evil Palamecian Empire, danger that must outweigh any personal good they could gain from a change of government. The Heroes of *Final Fantasy III* are trying to restore balance to the world because a crystal they found tells them that it is their duty to do so—taking advice from a crystal may be a strange decision, but their quest is an altruistic one. The Dark Knight Cecil Harvey of *Final Fantasy IV* starts the game secure in a prestigious job working for an evil king, then loses it all by developing a conscience and deciding to be a Hero.

Hobbes might be a little more approving of the wanderer Bartz from *Final Fantasy V.* Bartz is trying to save the world from the Wizard Exdeath. That may sound altruistic, but if Bartz fails to prevent Exdeath's return, everything on the planet will die, including himself. It is absolutely in Bartz's best interests, then, to prevent Exdeath's return. We might try to paint Bartz as a Hobbesian hero, letting nothing stand in the way of his quest to do what is best for himself. Even before Bartz is given this quest, however, we have seen him twice risk his life to save strangers from attacking Goblins, so there is no question where his real priorities lie. *Final Fantasy VI* focuses again on political rebels who are risking far more than they can hope to gain personally from a revolution.

Final Fantasy VII is a particularly tricky and interesting case. Its main protagonist is, of course, the famous Cloud Strife, the idol of an army of cosplayers and anyone else who loves implausibly large swords.[3] Cloud likes to play his cards close to the vest and never quite makes his motivations clear. As the game begins, Cloud seems the perfect Hobbesian, dedicated to using his gifts for personal benefit by selling his skills as a mercenary. Then he gets involved in the resistance group AVALANCHE, and things get murkier. He devotes himself to opposing the evil Sephiroth, but why? Is it because if Sephiroth is not thwarted, he will gain godlike power over everyone, and Cloud is simply protecting his own freedom? Is it because Cloud wants revenge for the way Sephiroth manipulated his memories or for Sephiroth's murder of the flower girl Aeris? Or does Cloud, behind the cynicism, really want to protect the people of the world Gaia from an awful fate? We simply don't know. Let's assume that Hobbes gives Cloud a nod of approval, if only because Hobbes is self-interested enough not to want a Buster Sword to the face.

Squall Leonhart from *Final Fantasy VIII* just goes from bad to worse in the Hobbesian model. He starts the game obsessed with doing his duty at the military academy, and as if that weren't bad enough, his friendships with Irvine Kinneas, Quistis Trepe, Selphie Tilmitt, and Zell Dincht and especially his romance with Rinoa Heatilly gradually transform him into a caring and giving individual. The thief Zidane Tribal from *Final Fantasy IX* is a hopeless case right from the start, with the personal motto "you don't need a reason to help people." In *Final Fantasy X*, it may be in Tidus's best interests for the demonic Sin to be destroyed before it strikes again, but Tidus stays loyal to this quest even when he learns that Sin's destruction would cause his own death. The Summoner Yuna from the same game is just as bad. At the start of the game she is already intending to sacrifice her life to combat Sin, and although she does become less enamored with the idea of dying as the plot unfolds, her main reason for choosing a less terminal approach is that sacrificing her life simply wouldn't be very effective. Finally, Princess Ashe of *Final Fantasy XII* may be striving to recapture her lost Dalmascan throne, which seems self-interested enough, but she's clearly doing it because she doesn't want her people to be oppressed by the Archadian Empire and she wants to put an end to the fighting. So yet another Hero fails to pass Hobbes's standard. Of course, there are many more playable characters in *Final Fantasy* games than I have mentioned here, but the trend is clear enough. These tales may be fantasies for some, but for Hobbes, they are nightmares.

As if the protagonists weren't contemptible enough in Hobbes's eyes for their lack of self-interest, he would also think them fools for their defiance of authority. As you know, Hobbes was in favor of monarchy and recommended strict obedience to the monarch. Yet showing strict obedience to the authorities is the last characteristic we can expect to find in a *Final Fantasy* hero. Hobbes would be horrified at the rebels of *Final Fantasy II* who fight to overthrow the Palamecian Empire, the rebels of *Final Fantasy VI* who fight to overthrow the empire of Gestahl, and the members of AVALANCHE from *Final Fantasy VII* who fight to overthrow the all-powerful Shinra corporation. Even the rebels who support Princess Ashe's return to the throne in *Final Fantasy XII* would be condemned, despite the fact that Ashe used to be the absolute ruler and was owed complete loyalty by the people of Dalmasca. Ashe no longer rules, so she doesn't count anymore. It is the Archadian emperor Gramis who rules in Dalmasca at the time of *Final Fantasy XII*, and so it is to him that the Dalmascans now owe their loyalty.

Interestingly, although the protagonists of the solo *Final Fantasy* games are generally abysmal failures by Hobbes's standards, the player-characters of *Final Fantasy XI Online* usually live lives that Hobbes would highly approve of. *Final Fantasy XI Online* is a MMORPG, a Massive Multiplayer

Online Role-Playing Game, a shared virtual world where players take on the roles of adventuring characters, often cooperating to meet common goals. Like player-characters in most MMORPGs, they work hard to increase their personal wealth and power, gathering loot and gils and advancing in levels through experience. Even Monks aren't above demanding that they get their fair share of the treasure. Whereas the protagonists of solo *Final Fantasy* games are generally dedicated to helping the world, player-characters in *Final Fantasy XI Online* seem generally dedicated to mugging monsters for the experience and treasure. It is true, Hobbes did say that it was only reasonable to avoid danger, but the player-characters are never really in terrible danger. They must surely know that death is not permanent in their world and that at worst, it means a trip back to their home point and the loss of a little experience.

You might think that I'm being too cynical about the characters' motives here. After all, even if they do seek treasure, they are frequently engaging in missions and quests that will help other people. Player-characters can be found doing things like helping bakers light their ovens, finding medicine to cure sick travelers, rescuing adventurers held captive by the Sahagin, and, of course, slaying lots of monsters that are plaguing people. Might not such activities indicate something of an altruistic streak? Maybe. It all depends on whether the character is doing it to build a reputation or doing it for the sake of helping others, and only the player knows that. Of course, not all quest-givers are equally in need of saving. If player-characters are as quick to help Professor Koru-Moru find an ancient alchemical text to satisfy his curiosity as they are to help poor Maloquedil get some garlic so that he isn't killed by vampires, then it would be hard to take protestations of altruism seriously. If player-characters are just as eager to help the cat burglar Nanhaa Migho fence stolen goods, we should be safe in concluding that they quest because of what they can gain from questing, a motivation that Hobbes would approve of wholeheartedly.

Even more revealing is what the missions and the quests accepted by a character tell us about the character's relationship with the authorities. National missions are taken on behalf of the authorities, so even when they require the player-character to bend the law a little, such as on an espionage mission, the character is still acting in obedience to the state. Some missions on behalf of national authorities, however, are undertaken in defiance of even higher authorities. For instance, the Windurst minister Ajido-Marujido requires the player-characters to engage in missions behind the back of his superior, the Star Sybil, a violation so serious that she is willing to kill him for it. Some quests even require the player-character to engage in good old-fashioned, greed-motivated crime. For example, the quest "A Job for the Consortium" requires one to smuggle illegal Brugaire goods into Jeuno, while the quest "A Moral Manifest?" requires one to help the thief Hooknox steal treasure from the Yagudo family vaults. Characters who refuse to take quests that break the rules might be considered by Hobbes to be acting reasonably. As for the rest, which I think is the vast majority of player-characters, Hobbes would be horrified at their lawless ways.

Before moving on from Hobbes, let's have a look at what he would say about the *players* of the online game. *Final Fantasy XI Online* gives the players unprecedented freedom (for a *Final Fantasy* game) to do whatever they want, and because their actions can have an impact on other real human beings playing in the same virtual world, there are very real moral choices for the players to make. Are the players acting strictly in accordance with self-interest in their interactions with other humans, unmoved by anything except what they can get out of people? Some of them are. There are players online who wouldn't spare a second to help a noob under any circumstances, players who will claim but not kill a Notorious Monster in order to make it respawn at a more convenient time, players who will try to block access to a Notorious Monster unless a toll is paid, even players who will engage in price-fixing at the auction houses. On the other hand, there are players who will take the time to patiently explain features to new players, even when the new players have to be told repeatedly before they get it. There are players who will wander through low-level areas with their high-level characters, just in case anyone needs to be saved from monsters. There are even players who, on rare occasions, will simply give items to strangers to help them out. In virtual environments, as in real ones, some people are motivated by self-interest and some are not.

Another thing that people do in virtual, as well as real, environments is break the rules. In the context of *Final Fantasy XI Online*, the "monarch" and ultimate authority is the Square Enix corporation, which owns *Final Fantasy*. The official *Final Fantasy XI Online* Web site keeps a record of accounts that have been banned by Square Enix for violations of the rules, such as "griefing" (playing a game simply to harass other players), the use of third-party tools, or making real money from goods or services provided within the game. Hobbes would conclude that the owners of such accounts were acting immorally and contrary to their own self-interests in breaking the "law," and they got what was coming to them. After all, when people decide to play *Final Fantasy XI Online*, they enter into a contract, agreeing (by clicking "I agree" on the user agreement) to submit to the rules laid down by Square Enix. All players give up certain freedoms, such as the freedom to grief people or to fight with other player-characters, for the common good, Not every player likes every rule or judgment call, but they all pay their monthly subscription fee to play in a world where everyone must abide by the rules. Once the social contract has been entered into, Hobbes would think that it makes no sense to live outside the rules and bring the wrath of the authorities down on your head.

John Stuart Mill Rides the Chocobo

Something bothers me. I think it's your way of life.
You don't get paid. You don't get praised. Yet, you still
risk your lives and continue on your journey. Seeing
that makes me . . . it just makes me think about my life.

—Reeve Tuisti, *Final Fantasy VII*

John Stuart Mill had a radically different take on the sort of life
a human being should live, and he would see the characters and
the players of *Final Fantasy* games very differently. Mill was
of the opinion that we should act in whatever way will produce the best consequences for as many people as possible.
More specifically, we should live in whatever way will best promote happiness and combat unhappiness. All pleasure is good
in itself, but some pleasures are more valuable than others, not
because of how intense or pleasurable they are but because
they are of a finer quality. In particular, pleasures of the mind,
the cultural and intellectual pleasures that engage our mental
faculties, are more valuable than sensual pleasures and other
pleasures that do not tax our intellects. So, for example, the
pleasure to be gained from reading great poetry or studying philosophy is superior to the pleasure to be gained from
food, sex, or games of chance. Mill labeled the more valuable,
intellectual pleasures "higher pleasures" and the less valuable,
nonintellectual pleasures "lower pleasures." So, in the context
of *Final Fantasy*, studying magic to learn the secrets of the universe would count as a higher pleasure, while munching roast
Chocobo, hunting Antlions, or simply enjoying the thrill of
combat would be only lower pleasures.

Mill's view, with its emphasis on pleasure, might at first
sound like a selfish one. On closer examination, however, it
turns out that the best sort of life in this model is unselfish in
the extreme. Mill thought that nobody's happiness or unhappiness is more important than anyone else's. This means that we

shouldn't choose to make ourselves happy if we can instead bring *more* happiness to someone else. So, for example, let's imagine that you have saved up just enough money to buy the new *Final Fantasy* game. Buying the game is a worthwhile use of your money because it will bring you pleasure, but because you could more effectively bring happiness to the world by giving the money to someone in desperate poverty, it would be a much better use of your money to give it away. Unless our lives are truly horrid, we can almost always increase the happiness of others more effectively than we can increase our own, and so we should almost always be directing our efforts toward the well-being of other people. Naturally, all of this would apply within the gameworlds of *Final Fantasy*, too. It will rarely be right for characters to do something for themselves, whether it is buying a new sword, seeking an old flame, or simply standing and admiring the scenery in Windurst Woods. After all, given the number of people who need rescuing in the typical *Final Fantasy* world, there is always something else the character could be doing that would bring more happiness into the world. If Mill's philosophy interests you, have a look at his book *Utilitarianism*.[4]

Though Hobbes would have judged the protagonists of the solo *Final Fantasy* games to be miserable failures, Mill would consider them shining examples of the way human beings should live their lives. The very altruism that Hobbes would condemn would earn only praise from Mill. After all, if we should always act in order to bring about the greatest happiness and relieve the most suffering, we can't go about it much more effectively than by saving the world. It is true, the heroes of *Final Fantasy* games sometimes have powerful personal feelings of guilt, depression, bitterness, or angst (Cecil Harvey, Cloud Strife, and Basch fon Rosenburg, just for example). It is true that heroes of *Final Fantasy* adventures always have to endure tough adventures with few comforts, adventures in which they suffer injury or even death. It is also true that an adventurer's life usually leaves little time for the intellectual "higher" pleasures that Mill values so much. We are not to treat our own happiness as more important than anyone else's, however, and the good these Heroes do seems to far outweigh any personal suffering they might go through. Cloud Strife may spend too much time obsessing darkly about his mysterious past, but he saves an entire planet from being enslaved by Sephiroth. Mill wouldn't even care whether Cloud's motivation is to save himself or take revenge, rather than to bring happiness to people. All that concerns Mill is whether the consequence of Cloud's actions is a happier world. So, too, for all of the other protagonists, the bottom line is that planets are returned to balance, wars are stopped, and evil tyrants are overthrown, much to the benefit of people in general.

Determining what Mill would say about the player-characters of *Final Fantasy XI Online* is a trickier matter. The first thing to note is that almost all of the characters compulsively undertake quests and missions, and most of the quests and missions require their helping people. As already noted, certain grayer quests involve stealing or smuggling, but on the whole, the life of an adventurer seems to be a life spent making the world a happier place. It may well be that the *reason* the characters undertake the quests isn't that they want to help people, but that it is the most effective route for personal advancement. Mill wouldn't care. All that matters is the fact that they make the world a happier place.[5]

Of course, undertaking missions and quests isn't the only way to advance in the world. One alternative is simply to hit the wilderness and start "grinding," slaughtering any monster you can find for treasure and experience. Sometimes it is plausible that this grinding is helping the people of Vana'diel. For example, it seems likely that clearing Giant Grubs from the vicinity of the town of Bastok is to the benefit of the Humes and the Galka who live there. On the other hand, sometimes it seems that the grind represents pointless animal cruelty, rather than a positive social contribution. One can slaughter the dinosaurlike Sarumugue Skinks of Aragoneu, but the poor animals, though fierce, don't seem to be doing a lot of harm except to the bats they prey on. More problematic yet, the many races of beastmen that the characters carve their way through seem to have a good claim on being people themselves. If Humes, Elvaan, Galka, Mithra, and Tarutaru all count as people, and I think it is clear that they are supposed to, then the same should presumably go for races like the Gigas, the Mindflayers, the Orcs, the Tonberries, and the Yagudo. If these beastmen are people, then their happiness will be as important as anyone else's for Mill, and killing them simply for experience and loot would have to be one of the most evil things anyone could do. Even if they are mere animals, he would think that their suffering is a bad thing and something to be avoided. The player-characters might enjoy the hunt and the thrill of combat, but it is hard to believe that their pleasure is so intense that it outweighs the suffering of those they kill and any that the friends or the families of their victims might have.

Finally, there are some activities that player-characters indulge in that do not advance them in the world or help others or harm others or serve any practical purpose at all. Sometimes player-characters, like we real folk, simply fool around and have fun. The most iconic example must surely be the Chocobo races. The Chocobo Racing Association has branches in every hometown where player-characters put the Chocobos they have raised to the test or just stand and enjoy the show. There are a few gils to be earned for the owners, but the low rate of return compared to that of adventuring makes it clear that the point of the sport is simply sport. The same can be said of clamming, virtual tourism, and, unless it is undertaken on an industrial scale, gardening. Other hobbies and crafts that are profitable in principle are often casually pottered around with in a manner that has more to do with recreation than serious business. Such frivolity may not be particularly commendable in Mill's model, given the more important things that the character could be doing and the fact that none of the previous activities seem intellectual enough to qualify as higher pleasures. On the other hand, neither are these hobbies a waste of time. The mere fact that they bring fun means that the activity has some genuine value. That's good news for those of us in the real world who spend time playing video games.

In short, then, whether Mill would approve of the lives led by player-characters in *Final Fantasy XI Online* would depend on how they use the freedom the game gives them. They might be anything from magnificent heroes to the most wicked of villains.

So much for the characters. What would Mill think of the players? One interesting feature of Mill's account is that it implies that there is something good about playing games in the first place. Mill regards pleasure as something valuable in itself, so simply enjoying a session of *Final Fantasy XI Online* is a morally good act. But before you get too proud about spending all night leveling your Dragoon, keep in mind that just because there is something good about enjoying yourself online, that doesn't mean that you wouldn't be better occupied doing something else. However much fun you are having, it is a good bet that you could be more effectively making the world a happier place if you were helping the needy, rather than playing games. Worse yet, you will recall that not all pleasures are equal for Mill and that the intellectually challenging "higher pleasures" are more important than the other, "lower pleasures." How intellectually challenging is *Final Fantasy XI Online*? I suppose it depends on how you play it. Mechanically grinding your way through monsters is clearly a lower pleasure. Studying party tactics and calculating the best way to fight effectively, on the other hand, might have a better chance of being considered a higher pleasure. So might appreciating the game as a work of art, because Mill certainly regards some art as providing higher pleasure.

Of course, the fun any player gets is no more valuable than the fun gained by anyone else, so Mill is not simply going to be concerned with whether players are having a good time, but whether they are contributing to other people having a good time. Players who aid confused newcomers to the game will surely score highly by this measure. So will those who team considerately with others, being conscientious about their characters' contributions to the group and dealing with their comrades politely and flamelessly. The lowest of the low, on the other hand, would be the griefers, who deliberately try to ruin the fun of other people for their own enjoyment. So, for example, Mill would have contempt for those who slaughter or claim monsters they do not want, who block access to Notorious Monsters, who lure monsters to places where they will attack other player-characters, who wake monsters that other players have put to sleep, or who engage in any of the other nasty tricks players have invented just to annoy strangers.

Aristotle Conquers the Elvaan

> I'm not just going to find a job. . . . I'm going to be
> the best there is.
>
> —Cloud Strife, *Final Fantasy VII*

Aristotle has yet another take on how life should be lived, and he would have very different things to say about the characters of *Final Fantasy*. He stated in his *Nicomachean Ethics* that the best existence for anything is an existence in which it is performing its function well.[6] A knife that cuts well is being put to good use, because cutting is the function of a knife. Thus, the good life for a human being will consist of performing one's function as a human being well. To determine the function of something, we must consider what it does best. A knife cuts things better than anything else does, so we can tell that the function of a knife is to cut. What a human does better than anything else is to reason, so reasoning well is the function of a human being, thus a life of reasoning well is the good life for a human. Having said that, Aristotle doesn't think that reasoning well is the only important thing in life. Pleasure is worth pursuing, and being actively virtuous is extremely important. Even wealth and friendship can be important, if only because they help us perform virtuous acts. To take an example from *Final Fantasy*, the best intentions in the world won't get your quests completed if you can't put together an adventuring party of allies to help you.

Aristotle believed that we could determine which characteristics were virtues because virtue always lies in the state of moderation between an excess and a deficiency in one's character. For instance, if we are too confident, we are rash, whereas if we are not confident enough, we are cowardly. The moderate state between the two extremes is courage, so courage must be a virtue. To put it another way, imagine that you are playing *Final Fantasy XI Online* and your teammate charges every group of monsters she sees, drawing all possible aggro down on the party, whether the party is ready or not. Your teammate's character isn't being courageous. She's just being foolish. Similarly, if you have a teammate who runs away from every single combat no matter how straightforward, his character isn't being courageous. He's being cowardly and useless. Courageous characters will be those who have a moderate reaction to danger, who don't lightly put themselves at risk but are capable of standing their ground in the face of reasonable danger.

Before we can start a systematic application of Aristotle's moral system to *Final Fantasy*, we have to decide whether the races that live on Vana'diel have the same function as human beings on Earth. Aristotle never met a Galka or a Tarutaru or any of the other player races, with the possible exception of Humes, if we may call them humans. We don't know whether Aristotle would say that the nonhuman races have the same purpose that humans have or not. In *The Politics* he claimed that it is natural for Greeks to rule over foreigners, so he might also decide that it is natural for humans to rule over other intelligent species, but all we know is that we are supposed to be able to determine the function of something by considering what it does best. Does the size of the Galka indicate that its function involves physical work? Does the Mithra's natural aptitude for hunting indicate that hunting is part of its function? Or, more disturbingly, might it be possible that a race like the Tarutaru is better suited to thinking than the Humes are? If so, would is Humes be left with any function at all?

I'm going to take my best guess and assume that real humans and all of the player races are similar enough to one another, compared to other forms of animal life, that if Aristotle got to study them all closely, he would say that they all have the same function. After all, strong as a Galka is, what distinguishes it most from the majority of animal species on Vana'diel is its intellect, so I'm betting that its intelligence is its most significant characteristic in an Aristotelian model.

Whereas Hobbes would have regarded most of the heroes of the *Final Fantasy* games with disdain and Mill would have regarded most of them with admiration, Aristotle would come to very different conclusions about the various heroes. Just for starters, he would be concerned about whether they are living lives of intellectual achievement, and this will vary a great deal from case to case. Frankly, we often don't know very much about the intelligence and education of *Final Fantasy* characters. It is a fair bet that Sorcerers such as Strago Magus, Vivi Oranitia, and Yuna have studied hard and are learned beyond the technical details of casting magic spells. It is likewise a fair bet that poor individuals like Gau and Vaan or individuals who have devoted their lives to fighting, such as Cloud Strife and Zidane Tribal, haven't had a lot of time for study. In most cases, though, we are simply in the dark.

There is no question that most of the heroes have plenty of virtues that Aristotle would admire. Most obviously, they tend to be brimming with courage. *Final Fantasy* plots repeatedly expose their protagonists to terrible danger. In fact, there has never been a *Final Fantasy* game that wasn't focused heavily on violence, and the heroes usually get into more fights over the course of the game than any real people have had in their lives. The heroes also tend to be just, at least insofar as they are always opposing forces who are unjust. We might add that they tend to be compassionate toward those who need help, steadfast in their purpose, loyal to their friends, and true to their word.

These traits are not universal, however. For example, although Cloud Strife's character evolves somewhat over the course of *Final Fantasy VII*, he is often shocking in his lack of concern for other people. He is even at first uninterested in the ambitions of AVALANCHE, despite the fact that they are trying to help the entire world. Similarly, the military cadet Squall from *Final Fantasy VIII*, while dutiful and stoic, is cold and unsympathetic toward other people for much of the game. Similarly, the urchin Vaan from *Final Fantasy XII* supplements his income by picking pockets and so cannot have a particularly great sense of honesty and justice.

Other characters will fail against Aristotle's standard simply for having personalities that are too extreme. After all, for Aristotle, the virtue always lies at the point of moderation between an excess and a deficiency, so any characteristic that is immoderate must be a vice. What can we say, then, about the generosity of the average *Final Fantasy* hero, the kind of person who is prone to dedicating his or her life to a noble cause, even in the face of probable (and sometimes certain) death? How, for example, could the Summoner Yuna's commitment to sacrificing her life to hold off the monster Sin be at a point of moderation between a deficiency and an excess? If that were the state of moderation, what could the excess possibly be? Aristotle would have no patience for such selfless and obsessively driven people. He would be better impressed by someone like Princess Ashe, who is at least looking to gain a kingdom, as well as rescue one.

Like Hobbes, Aristotle would show much more approval for the lives of most player-characters in *Final Fantasy XI Online*. We can't say much regarding their intellectual lives, of course. Presumably, most Summoners and Black, Red, and White Mages have had a thorough education and most Beastmasters, Thieves, and Warriors have not. That is an assumption, however, and I cannot even guess at what sort of education is possessed by the average Bard, Monk, or Paladin.

There is much more evidence to go on when it comes to the cultivation of virtues. Although clandestine quests might show a lack of honesty and criminal ones might reveal a lack of justice, the average quest involves helping someone (a mark of compassion) or righting some wrong (a mark of justice), almost always in the face of physical danger (a mark of courage). Better yet, the player-characters don't usually seek to help others in an immoderate way. Far from being naive idealists, the characters tend to keep their own interests very much in mind as they perform their heroic acts. They fastidiously collect gils, loot, and fame, while choosing foes who will best give them the experience they need to improve their abilities. In fact, the idea that one must improve one's own position in life in order to better be able to help others would be very familiar to Aristotle. He might not have heard of leveling up in order to defeat ever more terrible threats, but he did stress that one can only practice virtues when one has secured the practical means, whether that comes in the form of wealth, friends, or the right set of skills.

Of course, those who choose to advance simply by grinding through hordes of monsters will rate less highly. They might have courage but can hardly be said to concern themselves with virtues like compassion and justice. Rather than acting in moderate self-interest, they seem to have become excessive in their greed, living only to increase their wealth and power. Such self-centered characters would be scorned by Aristotle even more than the obsessive altruists of some of the solo games would be.

That only leaves the players to stand trial. Like Hobbes and Mill, Aristotle would have little to say about the players in situations that don't involve other real human beings, although I'm sure he would advise that video games should be played in moderation, a standard that many of us spectacularly fail to live up to. His advice for how we interact with other human beings in the virtual world would be the same as for how we interact with them in the real world: behave virtuously in accordance with moderation. Some of Aristotle's prized virtues, however, simply can't be practiced by a real human in a virtual setting like Vana'diel. We can't genuinely be courageous, for instance, because we aren't really in any danger. Nor can we show real temperance to the imaginary food and drink of the game world. On the other hand, we can still treat other people with compassion and justice. Anyone who helps other players complete a quest, gives them loot, or simply provides information to help them orient themselves in the game is genuinely cultivating compassion. Anyone who refuses to do things such as cheat other players in virtual trading, take part in the forbidden trade in real money, grief others, or in any way deceive other players when arranging to team with them can likewise be said to be genuinely cultivating justice. As always, acting with moderation is the mark of finding the right balance. If you give away all of your loot to others, leaving nothing to equip yourself, then you have passed beyond the moderate state of compassion and have reached the excessive state of self-denial. If you refuse to go back on your promise to help a friend hunt Bogys on Qufim Island, even though a friend in the real world has suffered a tragedy and needs your help, you have gone beyond the moderate state of justice and reached the excessive state of rules-worship.

Doing Things Your Way.
Ghaa Haah Hah Hah!

> Now I'm doing things my way! Ghaa haah hah hah!
>
> —Heidegger, *Final Fantasy VII*

So, who is right about the sort of life that we ought to live? Hobbes, Mill, Aristotle, or none of the above? That is for you to decide. I've got my opinion, of course, but the point of this chapter isn't for me to foist my views on you. The point of the chapter is to help you think through the issue for yourself. Maybe, as we considered these worlds through the eyes of the philosophers, you thought that one or more of them showed some insight into the purpose of life. Or maybe you thought they all showed about as much sense as a first-level White Mage charging a herd of Adamantoise with a stick. Either way, you have hopefully been given some food for thought while you struggle, as I do, with the question of what sort of lives we should live. We've scratched the surface here, and the rest is up to you. Working out the purpose of human life is no easy task, of course, nor will it be achieved quickly. After all, a great quest is always a long and difficult affair. But you knew that.

NOTES

1. Thomas Hobbes, *Leviathan*, ed. K. C. A. Gaskin (Oxford: Oxford University Press, 2009), pp. 84, 85.

2. I recommend the edition of Hobbes's *Leviathan* cited above. If you are interested in having a look at an excellent collection of essays on Hobbes, I recommend Patricia Springborg, ed., *The Cambridge Companion to Hobbes's Leviathan* (Cambridge: Cambridge University Press, 2007). The creature "Leviathan" from *Final Fantasy III, IV, V, VII, VIII, IX,* and *XI* is a reference to the same monster from Jewish and Christian literature, a

beast that appears five times in the Bible. The fact that Leviathan becomes a king in the *Final Fantasy* series is perhaps a nod to Hobbes.

3. Cosplayers, in case you don't know, are people who like to dress up as their favorite characters from anime, manga, or video games. The practice is most common in Japan.

4. An edition that I recommend is: John Stuart Mill, *Utilitarianism* (Indianapolis: Hackett Publishing Company, 2002). For an excellent collection of essays on Mill's philosophy, I recommend Henry West, ed., *The Blackwell Guide to Mill's Utilitarianism* (Malden, UK: Blackwell Publishing, 2006).

5. Attentive gamers will notice that even after a quest has been completed, the quest still remains available for other players to complete. If we take this at face value, it would indicate that while perhaps hundreds of thousands of people take the quest, the poor quest-giver is never actually helped. No matter how often someone brings Kuoh medicine for her sick Chocobo, the bird is still sick when the next adventurer turns up. This raises some interesting philosophical issues about how we are supposed to interpret the shared story presented to the player by MMORPGs like *Final Fantasy XI Online*, but I don't have space to open that can of Sand Worms here. I'm just going to assume that we are supposed to accept that the characters we play are the only characters who have ever really completed the quest. The alternative seems to be that everyone in Vana'diel is thoroughly insane for constantly trying to solve problems in a world that doesn't allow problems to be solved.

6 . The *Nicomachean Ethics* is an excellent book to read if Aristotle's ethics interest you. An edition I recommend is Aristotle, *Aristotle: Nicomachean Ethics*, translated by Roger Crisp (Cambridge: Cambridge University Press, 2000). For a wonderful collection of essays on Aristotle's philosophy, I recommend Jonathan Barnes, ed., *The Cambridge Companion to Aristotle* (Cambridge: Cambridge University Press, 1995).

THE FOUR WARRIORS OF LIGHT SAVED THE WORLD, BUT THEY DON'T DESERVE OUR THANKS

Nicolas Michaud

The world is veiled in darkness. The wind stops, the sea is wild, and the earth begins to rot. The people wait, their only hope, a prophecy . . . . "When the world is in darkness, Four Warriors will come."[1]

These are the words of Lukahn, a Sage in the world of the first *Final Fantasy*. His vision of the future is a bleak one, but he also knows that Four Heroes will come to fight the darkness. As the many incarnations of *Final Fantasy* have come and gone, the Heroes of the worlds of *Final Fantasy* have gained a great deal of freedom. Specifically, in recent versions of the game they can choose to save the world . . . or not. But in their 8-bit beginnings, the Heroes were predestined to save the world. In the first *Final Fantasy*, the Sage Lukahn's prophecy tells of the "Four Warriors of Light" who will come in the time of darkness to save them all. I can't help but wonder, then, if it was foreseen that these Four Warriors would save the world, do they really deserve our thanks?[2]

All right, that may seem like a weird thing to ask. "Of course, you should thank someone who saves the world!" you might reply. But to know whether we should thank the Warriors for saving the world, we need to know whether they have free will. If they don't have free will and have no choice but to save the world, then why thank them? Why thank someone who has no choice but to do something?

If the Sage Can See It All, Are the Heroes Really Free?

Many philosophers argue that someone is free when he or she has the ability to do something else. In other words, a person is free only if he or she can actually make a choice to do or not to do something. If a person is placed on a path from which he or she cannot deviate, then that person is not free. Predestination does exactly this; the Warriors of Light cannot do anything other than what they are predestined to do. If they are predestined, then they have no alternative possibilities. And here is the problem: don't we usually say that if people don't have free will, then they can't be praised or blamed for their actions? If I am enchanted by an evil Mage and forced to commit an action, good or bad, can I really be held responsible? Similarly, if the world is destroyed and there was nothing I could have done to stop it, can I really be blamed? After all, there was *nothing* I could do to stop it. On the other hand, if I save the world, and once again if I could do *nothing* to change that fact, why would I be praised for my action?

For example, I don't thank my Nintendo Entertainment System for doing what it was programmed to do—like turn on when I push the "power" button. I don't thank my automobile's airbags when they save my life in a car crash; similarly, why would I thank someone who was powerless to do otherwise? Aren't our Light Warriors simply the pawns of fate, unable to do anything other than what they are prophesied to do? They can't change their path: the Sage has foretold the salvation of the world. He saw the future as if it was already past; it cannot be any other way.

From even before they were born, the Warriors were going to save the world. If the Sage was really good at seeing the future, then he knew enough to know that the Heroes would be born, he knew they would save the world, and, most likely, he knew that they would want to save the world. And if they were also predestined to *want* to save the world, then they couldn't have wanted to do anything else! Not only could they not fail to save the world, but they also couldn't be free to choose whether they wanted to save the world! The future has already been seen, and their part in the universal plan has already been written!

What If the Warriors Met God?

A classic example of the problem that our Heroes face is the problem that God may know the future. How can we be blameworthy for our acts if God knows what we are going to do even before we do it? If God does exist, and if God's knowledge of all things—even the future— is infallible (God can't be wrong, because God is perfect), then we cannot deviate from the path God knows we are going to take. So, how is it that we are blameworthy for our actions when our paths are ones from which we cannot deviate?

Some philosophers try to get out of this trap by arguing that we are not forced to do God's will, any more than the Warriors of Light are forced to do the Sage Lukahn's will. So, although God knows what we are going to do, or, in the case of the Warriors of Light, Lukahn knows what they are going to do, this doesn't mean that they are being forced to commit the action. The problem, though, is that this lack of force still does not provide them with freedom. Perhaps God is not forcing us to act in a particular way, but if God knows what we are going to do before we do it, we still are not free to choose to do something else. We are trapped by this foreknowledge. Although it seems to be a choice to us, it is still a choice that could not be any other way.

Thomas Aquinas (1225–1274) argued that there might be another way to address this situation. If the problem is that God knows today what we are going to do tomorrow, well, perhaps the problem is thinking about God as something that exists in time in the same way we do. Instead, Aquinas argued, God is present in all moments of time, at the same time. Imagine the center of a circle—the center of a circle is present to all points of its circumference at the same time.[3] Similarly, God may be present in all moments at the same time.

If this is the case, then God did not know yesterday what you are going to do today because for God there is no yesterday. In other words, God does not have knowledge prior to the event that necessitates that the event occur. Now, this is a little different from the problem that the Warriors have with the Sage's prophecy. The Sage isn't perfect, whereas God's knowledge is perfect. So, perhaps, the Warriors still have some wiggle room and they are not quite as trapped by the Sage's knowledge as we might be by God's knowledge. Nevertheless, if the Sage is right, and the Warriors of Light will definitely save the world, they are still trapped by his foreknowledge, and so they may not have free will.

If the Heroes Are Trapped, They Can't Be Blamed . . . or Can They?

The idea that we cannot be blamed when we can't do anything else is very important. We don't want to be blamed for things we are unable to change. This is why God's having infallible knowledge of what we'll do before we do it would be a problem—it traps us! More important, in the universe of video games, the Four Warriors of Light are unable to change the events that Lukahn has already prophesied. So, if we agree that we should not be blamed for events we cannot change, then we are also forced to agree that we cannot be praised for events we cannot change—nor can the Warriors of Light.

But what if we are mistaken about the idea that we cannot be blamed for things we cannot change? Although we don't like the idea of being blamed for things over which we have no control, perhaps we still should be accountable. Let's consider the following example: imagine that a heroic Red Mage, let's call him "Nick," is out fighting evil. As Nick casts his Fire spell at a monster, his friend the Fighter is thrown in the path of the Fire spell. Before Nick can do anything, the poor innocent Fighter takes the brunt of the spell. What would Nick's friends tell him when he confesses his guilt? It is unlikely that they will blame him. Nick's friends will tell him there was nothing he could have done to prevent the event. If it was true that he could not prevent the event, doesn't it seem that he should not be blamed? That's why we don't want to be blameworthy for things when we cannot do anything else. If we are mistaken about the idea that we cannot be blamed for things we can't change, then we may be responsible for accidents. Heck, you could even be responsible for things you do under the mind control of some sinister Mage.

So, you should not be blamed for things you cannot change, right? Then why would our Heroes be praiseworthy? After all, their destinies were laid out before they existed, and they are unable to do anything that can possibly change their fate.

Why Harry Frankfurt Would Still
Thank the Warriors

Don't worry just yet. It may well be that our Heroes will get the thanks they deserve. Although it appears that our Heroes must have alternative possibilities in order to be blameworthy and praiseworthy, Harry Frankfurt didn't see it that way. Frankfurt, professor emeritus of philosophy at Princeton University, who is best known for his work on Descartes and for his book *On Bullshit*, thought that we praise and blame people all the time, even when they are predestined to commit particular acts. Furthermore, he argued that there's absolutely nothing wrong or unfair about our doing so! We are not merely machines that are programmed for one destiny; we are persons who can make choices. Even if those choices are not free, Frankfurt thought we could be praised and blamed for them.[4]

In his article "Alternative Possibilities and Moral Responsibility," Frankfurt presented us with several examples in which he believes we would justifiably blame people even though they are in effect predestined to commit certain actions.[5] He first presented us with a situation in which someone evil attempts to force someone else to do his will. So let's imagine a *Final Fantasy* example. The character Garland, being an evil person, decides that he will threaten you with certain death unless you commit some heinous crime. Now, Frankfurt pointed out that this event could play out in many different ways. Imagine that Garland tells you that you have no choice whatsoever; if you try to defy his will, you will immediately be killed. What Frankfurt argued is that what really matters is how *you* react to the threat.[6] He pointed out that you can react in at least two ways: you can be someone who does what Garland wants only because of the threat, or you can be someone who does what Garland wants because you *like* it.

Frankfurt thought that part of our problem was our confusing the state of being forced to do something and the state of having no other options. It might have occurred to you when thinking about the God example, but there is a difference between lacking control over something and lacking the ability to do anything else. Frankfurt thought that part of the reason we panic over the idea that we may not have alternative possibilities is that we confuse it with situations in which someone else forces us to do something. Frankfurt argued that, of course, we should not blame people for things they do when forced—for example, when mind-controlled—but there are situations when we can, do, and should blame people for the things they do, even if they can't do anything else.

From this, Frankfurt concluded that if you are someone who commits the act only because Garland is threatening you, then you should not be blamed. But if you are a person who is threatened, but you also enjoy the crime and are glad to commit it, then you are blameworthy. In other words, the fact that you are unable to do anything else—because of the threat—is not as important as whether you want to commit the act.

It might have occurred to you, though, that this is somewhat problematic because you were never really, truly restrained in your options. You could try to fight Garland, even if you would surely lose, but, nevertheless, it doesn't seem as if this is the same thing as predestination. You are not truly without the ability to do anything else. The Heroes of Light, on the other hand, are truly unable to do other than they are predestined to do.

Frankfurt was ready for this criticism, though. After we were ready to acknowledge that he might have a point, he presented us with his strongest example. Imagine the following scenario: Garland wants your help to take over the world, but he would prefer not to have to coerce your assistance. So although he can force you to help him, he waits to see whether you help him of your own accord. Either way, however, you will help him because if you try to fight him, he will simply use his powers to control you and force you to do his will. This is a case, then, in which you cannot do anything else. Let's also imagine that he'd rather you help him without his interference. He doesn't want you to know that if you don't help him, he will force you. Well, what happens if you decide to help Garland on your own, and he doesn't have to do a thing? He never uses his power; he never mentions that he will force you. You just walk up to him and volunteer. Well, aren't you still blameworthy for helping the bad guy—even though you had no choice?[7] Remember, you can't do other than help him because if you try to avoid helping him, he will simply force you to help him. Here, you have a situation in which you have no choice but to help Garland, but it is possible for you to still be blameworthy. From this, Frankfurt concluded that you don't actually have to be able to do anything else to be blameworthy. Essentially, you can be unable to do anything but what you are going to do—you can be predestined—and still be blamed, or praised, for your actions. So, perhaps, the Warriors of Light do deserve thanks and praise.

According to Frankfurt, the only time the lack of alternatives has a bearing on moral responsibility is when it is the only reason why we decide to do something.[8] So if we are forced to commit an act, then we should not be blamed because the only reason that we committed the act is that we had no choice. But, on the other hand, if we act because we have no choice *and* because we want to, then we can still be praised and blamed. Frankfurt wouldn't blame you if you were forced to commit the act, or if you knew you had no choice. But if you acted for more than that reason, for example, if you acted both because you had no choice *and* because you wanted Garland to win, then you would be blameworthy.

Why Are the Heroes Heroes?

As the Warriors meet others in the world, those others keep pointing out that they are the prophesied saviors of the realm. It's not as if the Warriors don't know they are predestined to save the world. Unlike the example in which you help Garland, the Heroes know they have no choice. Remember, in the Garland example, you don't know about his power. You are blameworthy because Garland doesn't have to use his power *and* because you help him without knowing you are predestined to do so.

The Heroes aren't quite so ignorant. They fall into the category of both having no choice and knowing they have no choice.

So, are the Heroes acting *only because they can't do anything else*?[9] It might very well be the case that because they know they have no choice, they do what they do only because they have no choice. If they know that the future has been set for them, what reason do they have to fight it? Don't they meet the criterion of people who do what they do only because they can't do anything else? Imagine in the Garland example that instead of being ignorant, you know his plan: you know that if you don't help him, you'll be forced to help him. At that point, can you be blamed for helping him, even if he doesn't have to use his power? Why would you try to fight his will if you know you cannot win? If you know you have no choice, aren't you absolved because you are helping him only because you have no choice? In the same way, if the Heroes know they have no choice, aren't they unworthy of praise?

Can Our Heroes *Really* Want to Save the World?

Now we have a situation in which we have Heroes who have no choice but to save the world and who know they have no choice but to save the world. Do they deserve our praise? Maybe they are really happy to save the world. Maybe they are the kind of people who would save the world even if they weren't predestined to save it. In that case, can't we say they are praiseworthy people? Well, we have to start asking whether the fact that they are people who want to save the world is something that is also predestined. Can they be anything other than nice, world-saving people? Can we praise people for being nice who have no choice but to be nice? One wonders whether we are simply thinking too deeply at this point. But then again, isn't that the nature of philosophers and *Final Fantasy*, to think deeply? So let's conclude by indulging in some deep thought.

Should we praise the Warriors for wanting to save the world, if it was predestined that they would want to do this? In other words, can we legitimately praise someone for being good if that person cannot help but be a good person? We might be glad that he or she is a good person, but do we say, "Good job. Well done"? After all, it's as if the person is programmed to be nice. The option of being evil never presented itself. In real life, we are much more impressed by people who have to work at being good. Aren't we more likely to praise people who have to put effort into accomplishing something? Aren't we more impressed by people who can say no to temptation than those who are simply never tempted at all? If the Warriors of Light fall into the category of those who cannot be tempted, why praise them when the possibility of failure is never an option?

Consider someone who can't help stealing. If someone is unable to refrain from committing a crime, we often absolve the person of blame. That is the whole basis of the insanity defense. If someone cannot help but do evil, regardless of the consequences to himself and others, we put him in an asylum because he, unlike us, does not have a real choice. In theory, you and I can make a real choice to want to do evil or good. But both the criminally insane and the Heroes of Light lack this ability. Neither can want to do the opposite of their nature. Remember, if the Heroes have been foreseen, then they may have been foreseen as people who would want to save the world. This means that they are people who cannot want to let the world turn to evil. The fact that they want to save the world has already been predestined.

Can Phineas Gage Be a Hero?

But now we face an even bigger problem. Aren't we all genetically predestined to be nice or mean, good or evil? There is more and more evidence to the fact that people are products of their biology. Otherwise, why would people take medicine to change their mental states? If I am depressed, there is medicine (or a variety of legal and illegal substances) that I can take to help me be happy. There are all kinds of drugs that I can take to change my body chemistry and, in doing so, change my mood. So, if the only difference between a "happy me" and a "depressed me" is a small pill, maybe the only difference between a "good me" and an "evil me" is also just a pill away. Perhaps whether we are nice or mean is more a matter of our biology than it is a matter of our choice.

Consider the case of Phineas Gage, who was the victim of an unfortunate accident back in the 1800s.[10] While he was working, an explosion drove a spike into his head. Before the accident, Gage was reported to be a nice, kind, and charitable person. Afterward, though, many of his friends and family reported that he was a different person, mean and cruel. He was the opposite of everything he was before; the damage to his brain radically changed his personality. In fact, there are many cases in which traumatic brain injury results in personality change. So, much of who we are may be hardwired in our brains; if we could change our brains, perhaps we could change from good to evil or change evil people into good ones. Unfortunately, there is currently very little we can do to change our biology. Granted, perhaps we could produce a pill that makes people want to be nice, but if you were born evil, how do we convince you to take the pill in the first place? In other words, what could you say to Garland (aside from lying to him) to convince him to take the nice pill?

The problem for the Heroes of Light now becomes our problem. If my good or evil nature is something that I am born with, then I have no real choice over whether I want to do good or evil. The desire to be good or evil was genetically programmed in me without my consent or control. How, then, can I be praised or blamed for the good or the evil that I do? Not only may the Heroes not deserve praise or blame, we may not either! Even at my most evil or most good, I was, in a sense, predestined to be that way. And, so, in this way, I lack alternative possibilities, just like the Heroes of Light. It was decided for them that they would be good people. It may well also be true that it was decided for us, before we were born, by our parents' genetics whether we would be good or evil people. And if this is the case, do we really deserve praise or blame for our good or evil deeds? After all, we may also be unable to want to be other than what we are.

We realize that the Heroes of Light may truly be unworthy of our thanks because they have no choice but to be who they are and they have no choice but to save the world. And if you remember the storyline, you'll recall that, ironically, our Heroes never do receive thanks. Their final battle with Garland results in their being unnecessary and so their heroic deeds are unknown outside of legend. Unfortunately, if we accept this conclusion, and if we accept the argument that we are biologically hardwired to be the kinds of people we are, we are forced to accept the prospect that we lack the ability to be other than the people we are. So if you are like the Heroes of Light and are truly good, why should we thank you? After all, you have no choice. On the other hand, if you are like Garland, why should we blame you? Once again, you have no real choice.

Frankfurt told us that we can praise and blame one another, but that doesn't seem to be enough for the Heroes of Light, who know they are predestined. Even worse, now that you know about Phineas Gage, you know that, in a sense, you are predestined to be a good or an evil person. That fact may be enough to make you unworthy of thanks, too, if you are what you are *only* because you cannot be anything else.

NOTES

1. *Final Fantasy* (Japan: Square, 1987).

2. I owe my never-ending gratitude to my best friend, Chris Balestra, for his invaluable help with this chapter. More of the ideas than I like to admit I owe to him. Not to mention the fact that he is way better at video games than I am.

3. St. Thomas Aquinas, *Summa Contra Gentiles, Book One: God*, translated by Anton C. Pegis (London: Notre Dame Press, 1975), ch. 66, p. 219. Earlier versions of this understanding of God's relationship to time were offered by St. Augustine and Boethius.

4. Harry G. Frankfurt, "Alternate Possibilities and Moral Responsibility," *Journal of Philosophy* 66, no. 23 (December 4, 1969): 829.

5. Ibid., pp. 829–839.

6. Ibid., pp. 831–833.

7. Ibid., p. 836.

8. Ibid., p. 838.

9. Ibid.

10. Malcolm MacMillan, *An Odd Kind of Fame* (Cambridge, MA: MIT Press, 2000).

PART FOUR

SIDE QUESTS OF THE ENLIGHTENED

SHINTO AND ALIEN INFLUENCES IN *FINAL FANTASY VII*

Jonah Mitropoulos

> That was a scream from this planet. Didn't you hear
> it? As if to say . . . I hurt, I suffer.
>
> —Bugenhagen

An alien entity threatens the world of *Final Fantasy VII* (*FFVII*), and its influences have permeated the lives of all of its characters. Having been exposed to this alien entity, Shinra—the massive corporation doubling as plutocratic hegemony—begins to extract Mako (the planet's spirit energy) seeking the Promised Land (a place full of Mako energy). Unfortunately, Shinra's actions threaten the planet and all planetary life. From the very beginning of the game, the main characters identify themselves as renegades bent on saving the planet by committing acts of ecoterrorism, such as blowing up power plants, in order to destabilize Shinra.

While "going green" is certainly all the rage these days, why would Sakaguchi Hironobu and Kitase Yoshinori, the game's designers, create characters who rage against the energy infrastructure on which a video game depends? Though the game's imagined world ultimately reflects ecological concerns in the real world, it does not simply reject all notions of technological development. Instead, it evokes Shinto spirituality in the digital landscape of the game in order to encourage a symbiotic relationship between real-world human technology and the natural world.

Japan in *Final Fantasy VII*: "Watch Out! This Isn't Just a [Video Game]!!"

There is a difficulty, however, with giving a philosophical interpretation of Shinto in *FFVII*. The difficulty is that to speak of Shinto as a single, internally coherent religion, one that possesses a theological or ideological tradition alongside it, would be misleading. Whereas other religions, such as Buddhism and Christianity, have long histories of exegesis that both originate with a founder (Buddha or Jesus) and position themselves around a core text or set of texts, Shinto does not. Even texts such as the *Kojiki* and the *Nihonshoki* were never considered to be integral to the practice of Shinto.[1]

Being Shinto does not call for a person to affirm a specific doctrine. Rather, being Shinto means being part of a tradition (culturally Japanese) whose articulations are many, nonuniform, and mutable within its larger social and historical setting. Shinto is plural (meaning that there are many Shintos), and it is inherently assimilative (in that foreign influences help inform how it is defined).[2] But connectedness with nature is extremely important to Shinto spirituality, and in this game, we see that this advocacy for ecological cohabitation with the planet comes to define which cultural assimilations are appropriate. Just as planetary life thrives when there is biodiversity, Shinto syncretism models an "orientation in living" that encourages symbiotic relationships with other cultures. Thus, Shinto serves as the basis for my argument that *FFVII* encourages a symbiotic relationship not only with the landscape but also with foreign cultures. It is thanks to Shinto's adaptive and syncretistic characteristics that we can use it to examine the philosophical elements of a Japanese cultural product—such as *Final Fantasy*.

As we shall see, the fictional world of *FFVII* animates ecological concerns, as well as the preservation of Japanese thought. The main character, Cloud Strife, openly says that he intends to save the world from human exploitation and physical destruction. Less obviously, though, the invasion by an alien entity allegorizes concerns about a modernized, Westernized Japan. Still, the game does drop a number of clues that its conflicts parallel those of Japan. For instance, its imagined world is one that is recovering from a devastating war. Cid reminds Cloud that Shinra, the large *zaibatsu*-like corporation, was a wartime weapons manufacturer before it transitioned to energy.[3] With Article Nine of Japan's postwar constitution, Japan is no longer allowed to maintain war potential (weapons) of land, sea, or air. Likewise, Shinra left weapons development to pursue advancements in energy and technology.

Akin to Article Nine, the archipelago nation of Wutai in *FFVII* is no longer able to possess Materia and has transitioned from militarism to tourism.[4] Yuffie scolds her father, saying, "You get beaten once, and then that's it? What happened to the mighty Wutai I used to know?" Now, she complains, Wutai is "JUST a resort town. After we lost the war, we got peace, but with that, we lost something else." Her response resembles the frustrations that many Japanese feel toward Japan's rearmament. In addition, a man in Wutai recalls a legend in which their gods protected them. "But," he continues, "in the last battle, we didn't fare so well. . . . I guess our beliefs were based on nothing more than legends." Again, this parallels the prewar belief that the *kamikaze* were proof that the *kami* looked after Japan.[5] Not only does an allusion to *kamikaze* figure as Shinto imagery, but Wutai itself also exemplifies the Buddhist-Shinto syncretism left over from a past cultural invasion. Mount Wu-t'ai, located in China, is where Ennin (a Japanese Buddhist priest of the ninth century) studied with Fa-chao (whose name resembles Da-chao in *FFVII*) before he returned to Japan with new forms of Buddhism. So, although the game takes place in a fictional world, we should not hesitate to think of its philosophical dilemmas as Japan's.

Some images in the game have meaning outside their Shinto context. The idea that Aerith "speaks" with the spirits of her ancestors, the Ancients, for instance, is not necessarily unique to Japan.[6] Yet it certainly has a particular resonance with Shinto ancestor worship. Similarly, while many traditions have water purification rituals, we should first associate those seen in the film *Final Fantasy VII: Advent Children* (*AC*) with Japanese spirituality. *FFVII* is a cultural product, and its Japanese creators are, regardless of how they might define themselves, participants in a Japanese-Shinto "value orientation." As Ben Hourigan observed in his responsive essay to totalizing discourses on video games, "Violence and antisocial behavior in *FFVI–VIII* cannot be separated from their manifestation in Japanese society: the games both reflect it and reflect on it."[7] Likewise, *FFVII*'s violence against what is identifiably alien reflects and reflects on the notion that Shinto is a cultural value orientation that undergoes change when it comes in contact with foreign cultures.

To clarify, reactions to modernization are not altogether unique to Japan—in fact, they strongly resonate with a global modern subject that copes with cross-cultural exchange. *FFVII* and Shinto are not xenophobic, though one kind of Shinto, State Shinto, historically was. Still, by animating aspects of Shinto thought, *FFVII* enacts the conflict that emerged when Western economic and religious influences and modernization were introduced to Japan. In this sense, we can observe the game's conflict in two ways: as a metaphor for real-world ecology (saving the game's digital landscape from extreme technologization as representing concerns in real-world ecology) and allegorically, in that its characters must come to terms with an invading, alien presence. That presence, Jenova, figures as the introduction of Western, Judeo-Christian ideology to the Japanese spirit (*Yamato damashii*). The game's conclusion proposes that a solution to these two conflicts involves an assimilation of Western and modernized ideologies that is mediated by a Shinto respect for a spiritually infused planet.

Going *Kami*, Going Green

Understanding the terms *kami* and *tsumi* will help us perceive the Shinto elements of *FFVII*. Each term is notoriously difficult to translate, so I will attempt to describe concepts that surround them. We shall see that as ideas, they pervade most aspects of the game. To begin with, *kami* is often translated as "deity." Yet there are many instances where *kami* defies English definitions of deity. Floyd Hiat Ross, in *Shinto: The Way of Japan*, described *kami* as "that which is everywhere present in varying degrees, and it stands for that which is not entirely present or visible to people." In this sense, *kami* is more like a spiritual energy that permeates all matter. "*Kami* is in nature and man is in nature also, and *kami* is in man."[8]

Although *kami* can be very specific at times, almost like a deity, it is the notion that *kami* is a spiritual presence that I would like to borrow. When Thomas Kasulis said in *Shinto: The Way Home*, "As a human in the land of *kami*, one is a portion of the sacred; one is an intrinsic part of the *kami*-filled . . . world," we can immediately recall Bugenhagen's description of Spirit energy and the Lifestream in *FFVII*.[9] He says, "Spirit energy makes all things possible, trees, birds, and humans. Not just living things. But Spirit energy makes it possible for

Planets to be Planets." Such a philosophy does not privilege human life over nonhuman matter, as the two are interconnected and interdependent. As Ross argued, "Everything is divine, *kami*-like."[10] If one chooses to follow the path to this presence, he or she walks the way of the *kami* (*kami no michi*).

But following the *kami* way does not mean adhering to prescriptive dogma. Rather, Shinto encourages one to connect with the *kami* presence, which one finds, in its purest form, in nature. Even the construction of Shinto shrines prioritizes harmony with nature, in that the materials used must be entirely natural and taken from locations undefiled by human encroachment. We might compare this with *FFVII*'s hidden City of the Ancients. Not only is it inaccessible to humans (protected by a labyrinthlike forest), but its architecture is almost reeflike with coral shelves, scaled pathways, and large shells as buildings.

The game's cinematography captures the presence of a *kami*-filled world by exposing the player to the natural world's transcendence. Whether it is the Nibel Mountains with natural Materia springs, Gaea's Cliffs with its inhospitable temperatures and spectacular vistas, or a giant condor that expires on the birth of its offspring, the characters witness many natural processes that leave them speechless. And whenever something threatens the purity of these natural things, Cloud and his buddies mobilize to protect them. To understand what the threat is, we must examine our other term, *tsumi*.

Tsumi is often translated as "sin," for it refers to what is impure or tainted. Its meaning, however, is very different from Western conceptions of sin. Kasulis told us, "The Western idea of sin generally involves intent," whereas in Shinto simply contacting *tsumi* (that which is polluted and requires purification) causes defilement, "whether the person knew about the offense or undertook the action voluntarily."[11] The interesting distinction is that intent does not necessarily play into who might be affected by *tsumi*. Sephiroth, Shinra, and the other enemies of the game, as it turns out, are enemies in that they have at some point come in contact, either directly or indirectly, with the polluting force, Jenova. Even Cloud behaves like an enemy at various points, having been exposed directly to Jenova in Professor Hojo's lab. Jenova acts like *tsumi*, in that it is foreign to the planet and spurs those with whom it comes in contact to behave badly, out of harmony with nature.

To describe the alien Jenova's arrival from space two thousand years earlier, the game uses a metaphor of disease (defilement). At first, Jenova's arrival alerted the Cetra (Ancients) on impact by "making a large wound." Then, as Ifalna relates, "He first approached as a friend, deceived them, and finally . . . gave them the virus. The Cetra were attacked by the virus and went mad . . . transforming into monsters. [. . .] He approached other Cetra clans . . . infecting them with . . . the virus." Ever since, Jenova has sought to take over the planet's Lifestream (*kami* presence). Immediately after Professor Gast of Shinra rediscovers Jenova, "The use of Mako Reactor 1 [is] approved for use," connecting the alien influence to the development of industrialized capitalism and the overtechnologization that endangers the planet. The planet continues to live, but it is forever changed.

"Inside our bodies," says Vincent Valentine in *AC*, "we all have a current like the Lifestream. When alien matter infests the body, this current is what fights it off. Geostigma is what happens when the body overcompensates for its unwelcome guest." Just as in the game, the conflict arises when something alien disrupts the natural processes of a body. When the body is tainted by this defilement, it behaves in ways that challenge the planet's Lifestream (*kami*). Kadaj says,

> Mother gave me a very special gift: the power to fight against a planet that torments its people. She gave this gift to all her children. . . . You and I are brethren. Brothers and sisters chosen when we inherited Mother's

memetic legacy through the Lifestream. But the planet doesn't like that. It's trying to hold us back. That's why it has been racking our bodies with pain, filling our hearts with doubt! I will heal you. Then we will go to Mother. We will join as a family and strike back at the planet!

Kadaj proceeds to visually demonstrate this process of defilement by stepping into a pool of water, causing it to turn black. He then instructs the children to drink the water, transmitting the defilement to them and exacerbating their Geostigma.

As previously mentioned, the way one recovers from *tsumi* is by undergoing a purification ritual. Although there are lots of different kinds of rituals, the one most often practiced is purification by water. It can be as simple as washing one's mouth out at a special well or as complicated as *misogi*—walking into a pool of water under a sacred waterfall. In *AC*, the characters purify themselves of Geostigma by performing such a water ritual. As they come in contact with the Lifestream water, their scarring instantly disappears. By linking Lifestream to the purification of Jenova's influence, the mythology of *FFVII* advocates an ecologically Shinto conscientiousness as a solution for overtechnologization.

Tsumi as Cultural Invasion

The Expulsion Edict of 1825, issued by Japan's government, commanded that any foreign ship approaching land should be fired upon, no questions asked. Prior to this, Japanese thinkers defended national traditions such as the imperial line, but concepts such as *sonno joi* ("revere the emperor; expel the barbarian") evolved from being merely symbolic into being ideologically axiomatic. The state began to define being Japanese with this xenophobic ideology. Although the causes for this kind of thinking are complex, it is clear that they developed out of an increasing exposure to Western influences.

Western philosophical constructs such as capitalism and expansionism began to spread in Japan, upsetting the existing feudal system, but it was Christianity that many Japanese feared most. The Mito scholar Aizawa Seishisai, who pioneered the concept of *sonno joi*, asked in his *New Theses*, "Why are [Western barbarians] able to enlarge their territories and fulfill their every desire? Does their wisdom and courage exceed that of ordinary men? Hardly. Christianity is the sole key to their success. It is a truly evil and base religion, barely worth discussing."[12] As Bob Tadashi Wakabayashi described, "Aizawa feared an indirect Western takeover through Christian transformation, or what we today would call ideological subversion and cultural assimilation," and speaking to the political leaders of Japan, Aizawa used metaphors of disease to warn them of "the barbarians' cunning designs."[13]

In the same way that Ifalna uses the language of disease to describe Jenova (whose name resembles the Judeo-Christian name for God, Jehovah, and whose two-thousand-year-old arrival pairs up with the beginning of Christianity), so, too, Aizawa spoke of the Christians as an ideological plague. "They [Christians] win a reputation for benevolence by performing small acts of kindness temporarily to peoples they seek to conquer. After they capture a people's hearts and minds, they propagate their doctrines."[14] When Jenova comes in contact with the natives, it behaves in the very way Aizawa feared: cultural assimilation. Eventually, exposure was unavoidable, and Japan's rapid industrialization in the 1920s and the 1930s cemented a culture of capitalism. But modernization (a foreign value orientation) and its effects continued to instill fear in the Japanese.

Harry Harootunian wrote that "Modernism in Japan sought, therefore, to resist the culture of capitalism . . . and an emerging modern life that itself was constantly being buffeted by a process of revolutionizing production, chronic civil strife, and social and economic uncertainty."[15] But in the battle against this foreign influence and culture of capitalism, radical Japanese thinkers ultimately betrayed the traditional values that they sought to restore. In order to cope with the invading Western/Christian value orientation, they began to assimilate aspects of Western philosophies to form an "essentialist" Shinto. They ended up with a Shinto philosophy that resisted syncretism—a fundamentally different Shinto altogether. Aizawa, for instance, developed his concept of *sonno joi* by studying the Christian missionaries' efforts to proselytize, which often meant the total suppression of non-Christian beliefs. New Shinto thinkers constructed a *doctrine* of the *kami*, rather than following the *way* of the *kami*. Christianity's dogmatic influence on Shinto was altogether dissonant with its traditional manifestations, and the cultural effects of this shift were substantial. This kind of prescriptive Shinto helped provide a philosophical justification for war, as was the case with State Shinto in World War II.

The presence of a culture of capitalism and emerging modern life are all over *FFVII*. For instance, in the beginning of *Advent Children*, Marlene—Barret's daughter and the narrator for the introduction—recapitulates, "Because of Shinra's energy, we were able to live very comfortable lives." She adds, "But wasn't that because we were taking away from the planet's life?" The cause of this shift of living is very clearly the result of Jenova's influence. Thus, the game commences with an attack on a large capitalist corporation, an analog of the *zaibatsu* dominating early modern Japan's economy, and Cloud—last name "Strife"—is at the center of it. He, like Marlene and many others, is torn between the lifestyle that Western thinking offers and the native spirit that it threatens.

Like Jenova, Sephiroth's name originates in Western Kabbalistic spirituality, where the sephirot represent the ten emanations of an Absolute God. As traditional Shinto lacks any notion of an Absolute, Sephiroth's very name should warn us that he is the product of a potentially problematic syncretism. In the game, this translates into his two contradicting forms: first, as the violent response to foreign influence (when he assassinates a major capitalist figure, a common foe of the game's Heroes), and then as the voice of the foreign influence itself (when he becomes the Heroes' primary enemy). We learn that Sephiroth was made by Shinra's mad scientist, Hojo, who forced foreign matter (Jenova cells) into him as a fetus—a defilement that can be read as *tsumi*. Although Sephiroth refers to Jenova as his "mother," it was a human woman who carried and gave birth to him. That woman is Lucrecia. Her name carries the connotation of rape and reform, which directly applies to her role in *FFVII*. According to Livy, the son of the last king of Rome raped Lucretia, who then killed herself as a response.[16] The fruits of her suicide—her husband's revenge—brought an end to Roman monarchy and ushered in the republic. This is exactly what Sephiroth (the fruits of experiments in obstetrics) does to the existing body politic of *FFVII*—not only does he assassinate the president, but his actions ultimately destabilize the Shinra company.

In this way, the Lucretia metaphor might refer to a technological rape of nature that Cloud is attempting to purify. The consequence of Hojo's unnatural science produces the being who finds the means to endanger the entire planet. In other words, ambitious industrialization (the science inspired by Jenova) is responsible for the state of postwar Japan—its postwar constitution and postnuclear environmental problems (Sephiroth summoning Meteor). The problem is not so much that Jenova has made contact, it is the failure to cope with this contact that results in a negative overreaction. The game's solution, then, is to follow the way of the *kami*. After being exposed to the *tsumi* of her unnatural pregnancy, Lucrecia seeks purification in a very Shinto way. Just as one does in *misogi*, she secludes herself from society by a pool near a waterfall. There, she "purifies" herself in the same way as her namesake: by killing herself. Linked with Lucrecia and Hojo, Vincent has also contacted *tsumi*. While attempting to stop Hojo, he ends up as one of Hojo's experiments. "[His] body is . . . the punishment that's been given to [him]" for being unable to stop science's rape of nature. He even says, "Hearing [Cloud's] stories has added upon me yet another sin [*tsumi*]."

Just as *tsumi* in the game can be read as environmentally detrimental to the natural world, it figures in a cultural sense as well. After all, if Jenova is an allegory for Western thought (modernization, technologization, and Christian indoctrination), then the game must refer to its effects in such terms. If we recall, Kadaj refers to Geostigma as the inheritance of a memetic legacy. Vincent also calls it "The Sephiroth gene. Jenova's memetic legacy." Exposed to this memetic legacy, individuals become sick with Geostigma; once indoctrinated, they dissociate from their society (hence the zombie-like behavior of children influenced by Kadaj). In the game, Cloud says, "I'm fighting to save the planet, and that's that. But besides that, there's something personal too. . . . A very personal memory that I have." In other words, the foreign influence endangers not only the physical world, but something conceptual as well—his memory of Aerith, or his "value orientation" toward the Earth. Sephiroth's insistence that "[he] will never be a memory" suggests that in the view of the game cultural exchange can produce potentially permanent side effects.

Responses to Foreign Matter

Both *FFVII* and *AC* portray a number of solutions to the conflict caused by foreign invasion, but like essentialist revisions of Shinto, many of them are unproductive. Barret will later condemn his early ecoterrorism, confessing "that wasn't the right way to do things." Even Geostigma, as Vincent describes it, is an overreaction to the presence of alien matter. Perhaps the most dramatic reaction is Sephiroth's assassination of President Shinra, *FFVII's* embodiment of capitalist villainy. President Shinra tells Barret, "These days all it takes for your dreams to come true is money and power." Not only does President Shinra destroy an entire slum, but as he looks down on the destruction from a penthouse (godlike) view, an excerpt of Joseph Haydn's *The Creation* plays in the background. The particular excerpt we hear involves Adam and Eve telling nature that it shall echo their sung praise of God's creation. In other words, there is the ironic equation of destruction with Christian conceptions of creation and morality. So while the benefits brought by Shinra's (foreign-influenced) energy infrastructure are ubiquitous, President Shinra's assassination does not manage to evoke our sympathies. The game's characters agree, and for this reason they briefly believe Sephiroth to be a hero.

The assassination seems to be modeled after some high-profile assassinations in Japan's history—ones that targeted individuals who were perceived to be corrupted by Western thought. Inoue Nissho, a Japanese nationalist and the mastermind behind the most famous assassination plot, wanted to attack modernity and the corrupt elites who represented it. He believed, as Stephen Large wrote, that "If only the Japanese, who had been led astray by fallacious 'distinctions' arising from Western reason and logic, could awaken to the intuitive truth that all things in the universe were one . . . they would be empowered by this great life-force (*daiseimei*) to perform their historic mission."[17] Although this sounds like Shinto, it is really a distorted Buddhism bent on violent reform. The key here is that like Inoue, Sephiroth attributes social problems to modernity: Inoue accused the corrupt elites of sacrificing the public welfare for their own wealth, and Sephiroth blames modernity on Cloud's ancestors.[18] Inoue and Sephiroth may succeed in affecting the history of Japan and the world of

FFVII, respectively, but their essentialist philosophies fail to replace the more syncretic ones that underpin them.

We have already discussed some characteristically Shinto solutions in the world of *FFVII*, such as the purification imagery in curing the children of Geostigma and Lucrecia's withdrawing to the waterfall. It is not until the last two minutes of *FFVII*, however, that we see the game's most successful and overtly Shinto solution. Right when all of the Heroes' efforts seem in vain, wisps of Lifestream steadily and unassumingly emerge from all over the surface of the planet and head toward the disaster that's about to take place. The image is one of convergence and neutralization, not destruction and victory of one power over another. As three different forces (Lifestream, Meteor, and Holy) converge, the same image of Aerith's face from the beginning of the game flashes across the screen, suggesting that the way of the Earth (as Aerith's name shares a phonetic correspondence with the word *Earth*) mediates this convergence. We see her mediation, like Shinto, is not articulated but simply lived.

Because Lifestream permeates the planet, it resembles Shinto's idea of a *kami*-filled world. The problem comes when scientists and politicians disregard the Shinto notion of a *kami*-filled world in pursuit of selfish goals. The German philosopher Martin Heidegger (1889–1976), in "The Question Concerning Technology," said that with modern technology, we no longer perceive the sun as the sun or a river as a river but as resources with the potential to be put to work for energy storage and distribution. Perhaps this is why one of Shinra's chief advisers takes Heidegger's name.[19] By forsaking nature's sacredness, these individuals birth mutations such as the monsters at Nibelheim, the Sephiroth clones, and Sephiroth himself (in one manifestation, Sephiroth is a distorted angel with a wing for one arm). By adapting the way of the *kami* to the ubiquitous ideologies of globalization and the modern subject, however, not only can we address ecological concerns, but Japan can preserve its cultural heritage while evolving with the times.

By saying that *FFVII* invokes Shinto imagery, I am not saying that it attempts to reinstate the "old" in place of the "new." Rather, the presence of Shinto imagery acts as an invitation to the contemporary gamer to partake in its redefinition—and in turn, the redefinition of Shinto ontology—in relation to a modernized and technologized world. (For instance, *AC* replaces the image of the sinking Holy Materia in *FFVII* with a glowing cell phone.) Suggesting that Lucrecia alludes to technology's rape of nature is not to say that *FFVII* is antitechnological. There are characters who advocate a harmonious relationship between humans, technology, and nature (Bugenhagen, for example). It is when science and technology overlook the ecological value orientation Shinto provides that things go wrong. "I . . . was defeated," Hojo laments, "by my desire to become a scientist." Geostigma and Meteor, with their environmentally apocalyptic overtones, are instead the consequence of capitalist greed and belligerent technologization. Shinto offers a way to cope with this memetic legacy, by inflecting itself on modernization so that the two coexist, rather than remain in a state of conflict. In this way, both threats are resolved through a convergence of value orientations that reorients a progress-obsessed mentality for one of ecological cohabitation.

When the Lifestream appears at the end of the game and Aerith's face flashes across the screen, the game contextualizes an ecologically Shinto attitude of cohabitation within the historical memory of environmental disaster. We recall the real-life mutative effects of nuclear fallout and the casualties of war. Rufus reminds Kadaj that "The Lifestream courses through our planet back and forth across the borders of life and death. If that cycle is the very truth of life then history, too, will inevitably repeat itself. So go on, bring your Jenovas and your Sephiroths. It won't matter. We'll do as life dictates and stop you every single time." This is to say, by remembering the past encounters of different philosophical perspectives, *FFVII* replays the productive solutions of biological and cultural symbiosis.

NOTES

1. Although thinkers such as Motoori Norinaga—a seventeenth-century figure who revived the texts and advocated a cleansing of Shinto from its foreign influences—would read them as such. In addition, despite the proliferation of definitions for Shinto that say, "Shinto is the indigenous religion of Japan," I agree with John Nelson that readers should "be aware (as well as beware!)" of the problematic subtext in such statements (to what does "indigenous" refer?). So it seems dangerous to speak of Shinto as a philosophical framework, despite the fact that many compare it with religions that do possess long philosophical traditions. See John K. Nelson, *A Year in the Life of a Shinto Shrine* (Seattle: University of Washington Press, 1996).

2. Thomas Kasulis described Shinto as a way of life, an "orientation in living," and Ueda Kenji argued that "Shinto, in the most comprehensive sense of the term, represents the value orientation of the Japanese people in the various forms it has taken and the developments it has undergone throughout Japanese history—including contact with foreign cultures." See Thomas P. Kasulis, *Shinto: The Way Home* (Honolulu: University of Hawai'i Press, 2004), and Ueda Kenji, *Religion in Japanese Culture*, edited by Noriyoshi Tamaru and David Reid (New York: Kodansha International, 1996).

3. It resembles a *zaibatsu* in the way it wields considerable political power. The major of Midgar, Domino, confesses, "Actually, I'm mayor in name only. The city and everything in it is really run by Shinra, Inc."

4. Materia is one of the game's battle aids and in many ways is an analog for industrialized weaponry.

5. Though the term *kamikaze* refers to the suicide attacks of Japanese pilots, *kamikaze* ("divine wind") originated as a concept with the typhoons that protected Japan from Mongolian invasion in the thirteenth century.

6. Although spelled "Aeris" in the game, her name is elsewhere spelled Aerith. Wikipedia noted that the developers intended the name to resemble the English word *Earth*. I use *Final Fantasy VII: Advent Children*'s spelling.

7. Ben Hourigan, "You Need Love and Friendship for This Mission!: Final Fantasy VI, VII, and VIII as Counterexamples to Totalizing Discourses on Videogames," *Studies in Contemporary Culture* 6, no. 1 (2006).

8. Floyd Hiat Ross, *Shinto: The Way of Japan* (Boston: Beacon Press, 1965), pp. 32 and 33.

9. Kasulis, *Shinto: The Way Home*, p. 24.

10. Ross, *Shinto: The Way of Japan*, p. 19.

11. Kasulis, *Shinto: The Way Home*, pp. 47–48.

12. Aizawa Seishisai, *New Theses*, translated by Bob Tadashi Wakabayashi in *Anti-Foreignism and Western Learning in Early-Modern Japan: The New Theses of 1825* (Cambridge, MA: Harvard University Press, 1991), p. 200.

13. Wakabayashi, pp. 140–141; and Seishisai, *New Theses*, pp. 147–277.

14. Aizawa, *New Theses*, p. 200. Or again, "[The Western barbarians] all believe in the same religion, Christianity, which they use to annex territories. Wherever they go, they destroy native houses of worship, deceive local peoples, and seize those lands," p. 168.

15. Harry Harootunian, *Overcome by Modernity* (Princeton, NJ: Princeton University Press, 2000).

16. The game's spelling of her name is Lucrecia. To differentiate, I use Lucrecia to refer to the *FFVII* character and Lucretia for her Roman model.

17. Stephen Large, "Nationalist Extremism in Early Showa Japan: Inoue Nissho and the 'Blood-Pledge Corps Incident,' 1932," *Modern Asian Studies* 35, no. 3 (2001): 533–564.

18. Sephiroth says, "They took that which the Cetra and the planet had made without giving back one whit in return. Those are your ancestors." Sephiroth's story changes over the game, but it is interesting to note that it begins with an incorrect, idealized vision of the past.

19. It is also likely that this mentality is what gives Shinra its name. Rather than following a "divine way" (Shin-*to*), it seeks to capture the divine (Shin-*ra*).

KUPO FOR KARL AND THE MATERIALIST CONCEPTION OF HISTORY

Michel S. Beaulieu

Vivi Orunitia begins *Final Fantasy IX* as a nameless kid in the town of Alexandria. As he wanders around trying to figure out who he is and what he needs to do next, you discover that a theatrical troupe is in town and you have a ticket for their show. Though the ticket turns out to be a fake, you meet Rat Kid, who asks for your help with a ladder. Like most of the town's people, Rat Kid and you will watch the show from the rooftops. As you follow Rat Kid, you read a sign in a side alley that says, "Proletariat Patrons' Movement." You naturally wonder, Who are the "proletariat"? But the game doesn't answer this question directly. So we need a little help from our philosopher friends.

The Job System and Class Consciousness

The *proletariat* is a term most often associated with the writings of Karl Marx (1818–1883), who predicted a movement in history that would lead to the breakdown of capitalism and the establishment of a communist society (basically, one in which class-based conflict would no longer exist). This final transformation of society comes near the end of a series of historical epochs (tribalism, primitive communism, feudalism, capitalism, and communism), the defining character of which is determined by the clash between those who control the means of production and those who don't. At a certain point in each stage of development, the material productive forces of society come into conflict with the existing relations of production, and an era of social revolution begins.[1] Consider Marx's most famous statement: "the history of all hitherto existing society is the history of class struggle."[2] This means that society and history are understandable as a struggle between two classes: the proletarians (those who sell their labor) and the bourgeoisie (those who have wealth). Power in this struggle rests with the capitalists (another term for those who hold the wealth). Over time, however, the balance shifts as the proletarians become aware of their oppression and find common cause with one another to advance their position. The same holds true for the bourgeoisie, who will form alliances to protect their interests. The coming together will eventually develop "class consciousness," in which a group, acting as one, produces real historical change.[3]

Returning to the world of *Final Fantasy IX*, the Proletariat Patrons would be the class of citizens in Alexandria who must sit on rooftops and crowd into narrow areas to view the entertainment that the upper classes enjoy. The poster implies a certain level of resentment, a very public display of class tension. In fact, we see such class tension throughout the worlds of *Final Fantasy*. Steiner and other members of the elite have a clear disdain for those who are not part of their class. Despite being one of the "heroes" in one moment in the City of Treno, Steiner blames the oppressed for their lawless ways. In *Final Fantasy VII*, AVALANCHE, largely composed of elements from the laboring lower segments of Midgar, opposes Shinra. And Shinra's leadership clearly has disdain for its laborers, going so far as to drop the plate on Section 7, killing the entire population in an attempt to suppress any opposition.

The introduction of the "job system" in *Final Fantasy III* reinforces the class-based nature of the societies our heroes inhabit. Classes of characters are introduced, each with its own attributes and status. Although the previous games clearly had classes, *Final Fantasy III* allows us to become much more active in creating a customizable class-based society. We do not merely partake passively in such a society; rather, we reinforce our class prejudices. As a fan of Mages, I tend to treat them as the better class. Knights, on the other hand, I treat much like Thieves—laborers who get the job done but are not the leaders. The lowest classes, Moogles, are also introduced for the first time in *Final Fantasy III* (more on them later).

As Marx saw it, history is the story of the development of human productive power. In the preface to *A Contribution to the Critique of Political Economy*, he said, "It is not the consciousness of men that determines their existence, but their social existence that determines their consciousness."[4] The materialist conception of history suggests that human activity, rather than thought, shapes history.[5] For example, in *Final Fantasy XII*, Vaan's position within Rabanastran society is defined by both his relationship with the merchants of the city and, by extension, the Rabanastran relationship with the Imperials. As a "careful listener" tells Vaan, anything, including moving back into the city from Lowtown, is possible with money. Vaan's activities, like those of most heroes in the *Final Fantasy* series, are dependent on making gils. He does not choose the hunts, set the price of goods, or even set the standards for the licenses he must accumulate. Yet his actions shape society and alter his relationships and social standing. Early in the game, the caravans from Dalmasca Estersand or Dalmasca Westersand, on which the supplies for the city depend, will (if one believes the people whom Vaan talks to) ultimately end if someone (Vaan) does not defeat the Fiends blocking them.

Fiends and Feuerbach

In many respects, the act of playing *Final Fantasy*, an agreement that your characters can take action to change both their individual status and the nature of society, is in keeping with the Marxist conception of history. In his *Theses on Feurebach*, Marx argued that "the philosophers have only interpreted the world in various ways; the point is, to change it."[6] He added, however, that "Men make their own history, but they do not make it just as they please; they do not make it under circumstances chosen by themselves, but under circumstances directly encountered, given, transmitted from the past."[7]

Why should the Light Warriors in *Final Fantasy I* battle Fiends if the outcome will have no effect on society? In *Final Fantasy VI*, why should Cloud take on Shinra if their quasi world government is not going to end? Even Yuna's physical (leveling up) and philosophical (coming to grips with her impending death) preparation in *Final Fantasy X* to take on Sin (the embodiment of the ultimate rejection of an industrial and capitalist world) can be accomplished only through action. Only by actively changing the world can the social and philosophical problems our heroes face be solved. On the surface, while each game in the *Final Fantasy* series is unique and (aside from the rare sequel) its own self-contained plot, the stories and the histories they often develop or reveal are in keeping with this concept. Typically, heroes face a quest of some sort in a world wrought by an uprising or rebellion against an economic, political, or religious Power. Bent on maintaining its control over the world, sometimes with the desire to destroy it, this Power works to preserve its rule and view of how society should be structured and run. The player is often thrust into the action, controlling a character or group of characters

who band together in common cause and struggle against
oppression.

Every game eventually reaches a climax in which the main
protagonist faces off against the main antagonist, and victory
is achieved in some form. Notice that this change does not
have to be positive. In fact, if one assumes the Marxist position
that society will undergo a number of changes before reach-
ing a utopian existence, then it stands to reason that periods
of hardship will be necessary for progress. The end of *Final
Fantasy VII*, for example, is not entirely the positive experience
gamers may have hoped for (Aeris, after all, is killed and Midgar
largely destroyed). Similarly, at the end of *Final Fantasy X*,
change has occurred when Sin is banished for good, but it is
unclear whether this is a positive development.

"Champion of the Sewers Aspires to Noble Action"

For some of the games in the series, Marx's ultimate social
change—communism—is not even possible. As in Marx's
feudal stage of development, the political structure of many
of the games is defined by the economic relationship between
kings and nobility and villages and peasants. Often, members
of both of these segments of society partake in the quest,
so it is only natural that most of the games in the series do
not seek to dramatically alter the political, social, or even religious status quo. Instead, they seek to replace it with something
similar but more just. These endings, though, often speak to
an opportunity to move beyond. For example, although the
four Light Warriors of the original *Final Fantasy* seek to dramatically change the overall structure of the society in which
they live, at the end of the game, with the defeat of Chaos they
return to a social structure apparently unchanged politically,
economically, and religiously. They have, however, ended the
time loop paradox that had allowed Garland to live forever

and, by extension, had prevented society from progressing beyond its current stage of development. They have changed not only the immediate future (one, ironically, in which their deeds are unknown) but also any potential future.

Players like to believe that the heroes of many of the games are cut from the cloths of revolutionaries. Zidane of *Final Fantasy IX* is a Thief fighting against the upper class, which is represented by the abusive power of Princess Garnet's mother. Vaan of *Final Fantasy XII* is a poor orphaned resident of Lowtown, who, before the quest, can use only his labor (either through hunting beasts in the wastelands surrounding Rabanastre or in exchange for other odd jobs) to get gils. The character Dalan best expresses what the player thinks of Vaan's role in the game world: "[a] Champion of the sewers [who] aspires to noble action."

But, alas, many of the heroes in the *Final Fantasy* series, though noble, are not Marxist heroes. Their ultimate goal is to vanquish some badass evildoer, but they often have someone in mind as a replacement: themselves or another feudal lord. Some explanations, however, can be offered. As Marxism sees it, some individuals and groups of individuals may not be ready for a historical change—the social class has not attained enough "class consciousness" for the next stage of development. In *Final Fantasy II*, the four main characters (Firon, Maria, Guy, and Leon) seek to avenge their parents' deaths at the hand of the Emperor of Palamecia. To achieve this end, they join the resistance and eventually overthrow the Emperor. In *Final Fantasy IV*, we have the Empire of Baron that attacks its neighbors in search of four crystals. After one of the king's most loyal soldiers, Cecil Harvey, the leader of the Red Wings, begins to question his king (who we find out is being manipulated by the evil Golbez), Harvey sets out to destroy him. Harvey succeeds, marries, and is himself made King of Baron. Finally, consider the heroes in *Final Fantasy V*. The main character Bartz and three strangers set out to save the crystals that have begun to be shattered by Exdeath in order to release the Void, which will consume the world. The party defeats the Void and saves the world. In all of these games, the assumption is that the new rule will be benevolent and, perhaps naively, egalitarian—the "good guys" won, after all. But in the end, has anything really changed?

Moogles of the World, Unite?

What about the Moogles? First appearing in *Final Fantasy III*, they are the true proletarians of the various *Final Fantasy* worlds. In *Final Fantasy IX*, *Chronicles*, and the *Final Fantasy III* remake, they run a message service. In *Final Fantasy XI*, they are essentially vassals or serfs who take care of players' houses, change jobs, and run events. By *Final Fantasy XII*, they are tradespeople (mechanics, and so forth), while in *Final Fantasy IX*, they are cartographers, merchants, and so on. It is only in *Final Fantasy Tactics* and *Tactics A2* that they are active, but even then their fate is not really their own.

Players or heroes never consider the plight of the Moogles. Not once do the events that unfold in the game address the simple but natural question: is this best for the Moogles? Perhaps they are the real strength behind the Proletariat Patrons Movement and, as a result, should be the ones to begin a revolution. A nineteenth-century Marxist might reply, "No!" Just as each *Final Fantasy* game is truly its own story and world, the same can be said for the ultimate rise of the Moogle proletariat. It truly depends on the game and the unique circumstances surrounding its individual stage of development.

Much of the *Final Fantasy* series is set in feudal political landscapes, even if the trappings of an industrial world are present. It is not until *Final Fantasy VI* that the social structure and the social relations more closely resemble the nineteenth century. The game presents a society that develops technologically following the War of the Magi. But its main character,

Terra Branford, a human-Elf former slave, hooks up with the Returners, rebels seeking to overthrow the Empire. Terra battles the Emperor and Kefka (who kills the Emperor and takes control), and eventually the world is rejuvenated due to release of the magic.

The story of *Final Fantasy VII* is set in a world essentially controlled by the Shinra Electric Power Company. Cloud Strife and a diverse group seek to stop Shinra from sucking away the planet's life. Shinra's power allows it to act as a world government, with outposts on the other continents of the world to maintain control. But much of the story surrounds the city of Midgar, the industrial metropolis of Shinra. The upper levels of Midgar, where the upper class lives, are contrasted with the slums below the city, where the vast majority of the laboring class dwells. The slums, Sector 7 in particular, are the home of the resistance led by AVALANCHE. In the ultimate act of class conflict, Shinra collapses the upper plate of Sector 7, killing the entire population. All of this is backstory, however, to the plan by Sephiroth to use the Lifestream to be reborn as a god. Cloud is eventually victorious, although it is a mixed victory. While much of the Shinra executive is destroyed, as is Sephiroth (or so we think), Aeris loses her life, and most of Midgar is laid to waste and, as we learn later in the movie *Advent Children*, the poor become desolate and sickness runs rampant as a result of our heroes' actions.

Final Fantasy, Interrupted

It is curious—and odd—that the Marxist conception of history has found no fulfillment in any of the *Final Fantasy* worlds. While in *Final Fantasy VII*, we have perhaps the closest example of change occurring with the reaction against Shinra, most of the worlds have either rejected industrialization, such as in *Final Fantasy X*; are on the precipice of accepting industrialization, such as in *Final Fantasy IX*; or have only recently re-embraced it, as in *Final Fantasy X2*. Karl Marx wrote during a period of rapid and unprecedented change in the Western world, not unlike many of the worlds of *Final Fantasy*. So, why has the Marxist conception of history stalled in these (and our own) worlds? Perhaps it is because these societies have not matured to the point where a utopian existence is possible. While at the end of *VII*, Shinra may be rejected, capitalism as an economic structure persists. In *X2*, the readoption of large-scale industrialization is only in its infancy and only time will tell. If rumors are true, the soon-to-be-released *Final Fantasy XIII* will be set in a futuristic world. So, perhaps the Moogles and other oppressed folk in that world will be ready to embrace, dare I say, the final *Final Fantasy*.

NOTES

1. Preface to *A Contribution to the Critique of Political Economy*, p. 389. Unless otherwise indicated, all references are from David McLellan, ed., *Karl Marx: Selected Writings* (Oxford: Oxford University Press, 1977).

2. *The Communist Manifesto*, p. 222.

3. Karl Marx, *Capital*, vol. 1, translated by Ben Fowkes (London: Penguin, 1976), p. 344.

4. Preface to *A Contribution to the Critique of Political Economy*, p. 389.

5. Marx, *The German Ideology*, p. 390.

6. Marx, *Theses on Feuerbach*, p. 158.

7. Marx, *The Eighteenth Brumaire of Louis Bonaparte*, p. 300.

SIN, OTHERWORLDLINESS, AND THE DOWNSIDE TO HOPE

David Hahn

Final Fantasy X portrays a world plagued by Sin. The people of Spira cope with the existence of this overwhelming terror by placing their faith in the religion of Yevon and the Summoners, who allegedly are the only ones capable of saving Spira and of initiating the longed-for Calm. Although such a faith may give comfort to the Spirans, worldly philosophers such as Niccolò Machiavelli (1469–1527) and Friedrich Nietzsche (1844–1900) would find little solace in either the Yevonites' or the Summoners' belief systems. Both philosophers would lament the effect that the Yevonite religion has had on the population of Spira and would condemn it for encouraging the Spirans to place their hope in a false "otherworldliness" at the expense of their present lives.

Backstories

Niccolò Machiavelli is famous (or infamous) for his political writings, which include *The Art of War*, *The Discourses on* the *First Decade of Titus Livy*, and, of course, his most famous book, *The Prince*.[1] Machiavelli served as secretary to the Ten of Florence, negotiating foreign affairs and treaties. His career put him in touch with many of the most powerful and colorful persons of his day: King Louis XII, Pope Alexander VI and his infamous son Cesare Borgia, as well as Leonardo Da Vinci. Such contacts gave Machiavelli a unique perspective on how the powerful lived—and died.

Nietzsche's philosophical fame comes from his criticisms of Christian morality in the books *Beyond Good and Evil, Of the Genealogy of Morals*, and his most popular book, *Thus Spoke Zarathustra*. Nietzsche saw contemporary morality as the unfortunate reversal of the classical values of the Greeks and the pagan Romans.

The two philosophers had a similar goal: they desired a return to the spirit of action, a focus on this world, and a will to power. Both blamed modern religion for much that ails us. Their criticisms and recommendations not only applied to their respective societies, they continue to resound today, and they can even provide some advice to the people of Spira.

The Dream of Spira

A world without Sin. . . . That is the dream of all Yevon's children and we will use that power even if it means our lives.

—Isaaru

The dream of the absence of Sin is only a temporary reality. The Final Aeon cannot destroy Sin; it can only force it into absence. This period of time, the Calm, is worth it, nonetheless. As Tidus explains, "Even for a little while . . . people can sleep in their beds without being afraid. That kind of time is worth anything." This is the motive that drives the Summoners in their task.

Because the population of Spira values the Calm so highly, the Summoners risk everything to accomplish this task. The hope that the people have in the Calm is so significant that in the words of Lady Yunalesca, it "allows us to accept fate, however tragic it might be." Machiavelli and Nietzsche were both deeply suspicious of the belief that all suffering will be worth it because in the future that suffering will be rewarded. Whether the reward is true or not doesn't matter; what matters is the *idea* of it. Machiavelli, for instance, was not concerned with the question of whether Christianity was true; what concerned him was how Christianity affected people's political lives.

The people of Spira suffer for the promise of an otherworldly reward. They want the Calm, but the religion preaches something more. Beneath the veneer of the Calm is also the complete eradication of Sin, which can be accomplished by the piety of the people. They shun technology as forbidden, in the hope of this potential reward. But should they?

To answer that question, let's concern ourselves with the story of Wakka's brother Chappu. We are told during the adventure that Chappu was a Crusader, in the military branch of the theocracy, and went to battle Sin. Initially, he left with a Yevon-approved sword but defied the teachings, laying it down for an Al Bhed weapon (we can assume it was some sort of firearm). During the battle with Sin, he was killed. The teachings of the religion place the blame of his death on Chappu's use of a gun. Although Chappu's choice was a practical one (after all, a gun is a safer weapon for the user than a sword is), Wakka blames Chappu for his own death. Furthermore, Wakka uses the tragedy as fuel for his own fundamentalism. In fact, the very idea of an attack on Sin by anyone other than a Summoner is derided by Yevon as a reckless exercise in pride, outside of their teachings.

While the people of Spira rely on a future without Sin, Machiavelli's people rely on an existence without suffering after this world. This reliance on the incentive of heaven weakens a person's ability to act now. Even princes were unlikely to act preemptively or violently. Instead, they waited for problems to arise so that they could act with the blessings of the Church. Princes were concerned not so much with the state or the citizens but with their status in the next life. Machiavelli decried this, lamenting, "He who neglects what is done for what ought to be done, sooner effects his ruin than his preservation."[2]

According to Christian doctrine, wars are just only if fought according to certain guidelines (known as the Just War Theory). Wars of aggression are prohibited, and the violence of war should be the last resort, after all other forms of conflict resolution have failed. As a consequence, princes who wished to be good Christians would delay combat as long as possible (often to their detriment) and finally, when they did go to war, would hire mercenary armies to fight for them. This reliance on professional armies was often inefficient and dangerous for those who hired them because mercenaries fight only when paid, when it is convenient for them to fight, and when it is safest for them. Also, the mercenaries had a tendency to switch loyalties to the highest bidder. A prince takes a lot of risks when he avoids dirtying his hands with sinful acts.[3] We can see this in the attitude of the Maesters during Operation Mi'ihen. Maesters Seymour and Kinoc are both present for the joint operation between the Al Bhed and the Crusaders, but Seymour states that he is there not as a Maester but as a citizen of Spira. Although present for observation, the two cannot participate because that would "dirty their hands." This prevents Seymour from using his considerable power to aid the attack.

Whether in Spira or in Renaissance Italy, the reluctance of those in charge to take the actions necessary to their state's security remains a problem. The common threat, according to Machiavelli, is that religious indoctrination prevents those who fight from gaining the full support of their respective populations and government.

Striving for the Farplane

Life is but a passing dream, but the death that follows
is eternal.

—Maester Seymour

With few exceptions, religion teaches us that this world is
merely a temporary step in a much larger journey. What really
matters is the life to come. The quality of that life depends on
whether we live this life according to the virtues and values
proscribed by our respective religions. Nietzsche saw tremendous lost opportunities in this life-denying mind-set. Worldly
glory and accomplishments are not only ignored, they're transformed into vices by modern religion.

The old religions of Classical Greece and Rome didn't worship the meek and the humble but rather the accomplished. In
contrast, otherworldly religions such as Christianity praise the
characteristics of the meek and the humble, esteeming them
not because they make this life easier but because they guar-
antee the paradise of the next life. The old religions don't have
this feature because their afterlife contains no reward. The
Greek concept of Hades is not a place of eternal punishment;
it was literally just a house for the dead.

The other world for the followers of Yevon does not happen after they die. Instead, it is a hypothetical future in which
Sin does not exist. Still, there are important similarities. For
instance, the Summoners who have given their lives to defeat
Sin are revered in Spira as religious martyrs. The sacrifice of
life, the repudiation of this existence, is given the highest accolade. Any attempt to solve the dilemma of Sin while trying to
preserve one's life is viewed as a serious transgression. Thus,
after Yuna refuses to sacrifice herself and one of her guardians,
she is rebuked by Maester Mika, "Clad in it [Sin], Yu-Yevon
is invincible. And the only thing that could have pierced that
armor you have destroyed! Nothing can stop it now."

The death of the Summoner is necessary to destroy Sin, according to Yevon. Any attempts by the Crusaders, the Al Bhed, or joint operations like Operation Mi'ihen are doomed to failure because while people die in these attacks on Sin, they are not sacrificed like the Summoners. The Christian parallel is obvious: only through the sacrifice and death of Jesus can the doors to paradise open. This is why Nietzsche despised Christianity and all otherworldly religions: they focus on death and preach a resignation of this world.

The result of this negative attitude regarding this world is that the average Spirans cannot seek paradise for themselves. Unless they are Summoners, the most they can do is be pious and wait. Fettered by the precepts of Yevon, they are not allowed to use technology. Their religion has made them perpetual victims. Furthermore, they are taught that they are responsible for Sin's existence. As Yuna explains, "Sin is our punishment for our vanity. And it will not go away until we've atoned."

The vanity they must atone for was expressed in their use of machina. According to the teachings of Yevon, machina signifies Spira's contempt for nature, seeking to conquer it through the use of technology. As the party rides on an elephantine creature called a "Shoopuf or Shipāfu" Wakka points out a sunken city beneath the river and offers the Yevonite explanation for the city's original existence, "they just wanted to prove they could defy the laws of nature." He calls the city's destruction "a good lesson." Such indoctrination stunts the development of Spira because it imposes a limitation on intellectual development. Tidus is even rebuked by Wakka when he asks why Maester Mika hasn't retired at such an old age. Questioning the religion is not tolerated.

The Value Inversion

This inversion of the value-positing eye—this need
to direct one's view outward instead of back to

oneself—is the essence of resentment: in order
to exist, slave morality always first needs a hostile
external world.

Friedrich Nietzsche[4]

Because the Sin of Spira is external, developing a worldly
paradise is impossible. It is through this externality of Sin that
Yevon's theocracy is able to maintain such a powerful hold on
the population. For Spira, Sin is not an idea but a tangible and
terrible being capable of wanton death and destruction on an
apocalyptic scale. Faith in the Summoners and in the teachings
is effective because Sin is a graphic and real physical thing.
It makes the average Spiran more apt to imagine a world without the mundane evils, such as the pain, guilt, and suffering
that characterize most of our lives.

Nietzsche would interpret the Spiran situation as he would
that produced by Christianity, which, as he saw it, inverts
morality so that it plays to the strengths of the masses, rather
than to the strengths of the few. Otherworldly religions play
on the fears of the troubled masses in order to gain support
for a new way of thinking that would subvert the old hierarchies. In *Beyond Good and Evil* and *On the Genealogy of Morals*,
Nietzsche explained the overturning of values that has led us
to our modern conception of morality.

In the past, the classical ages of Greece and Rome, what was
considered good were the values of the nobility: those things
that were useful and that brought glory in this life. Anything
that was to be deemed "good" had to serve a purpose and serve
it well. Things that were lowly, wretched, and useless were considered "bad."[5] Our word *evil* did not exist for these people at
their time. Nietzsche, in *Ecce Homo*, called this "the great rebellion against the dominion of *noble* values."[6] Feeling powerless,
the common people revolted against the aristocracy.

They didn't revolt using pitchforks, Aeons, or machina
because they didn't have the strength or courage to.

Instead, they revolted by using a new mode of thinking that inverted the values of society. With the aid of the upstart Christian religion, they relabeled the values of the nobility, associating the nobles' conception of "good" with a newly created concept: "evil." At the same time, the traits that were deemed "bad" by the nobility were transformed into "good." Thus, the very things that were prized so highly by the nobles (opulence, extravagance, pride, and strength) were changed into "sins" (wrath, greed, pride, lust, and so on). The commoner's way of life— poor, weak, sickly—became the basis of the new morality. As a result, the highest value is placed on being the lowliest of people. This new morality encourages humility and promises a perfect life in the next world as a reward. In Spira, the obvious parallel is in the forbiddance of technology. Sin was created by a Summoner who feared that machina would wipe out his city; after a thousand years, the use of machina is forbidden not only in law but also in spirit. The only machina used is that of the Al Bhed, who are deemed heretics.

As Nietzsche saw it, otherworldly religions encourage us to deny our natural instincts in favor of an artificial moral system. This moral system asks for strength to be weak, which is "just as absurd as demanding that weakness represent itself as strength."[7] Yevon gives solace to the people that they would be free from the monster Sin, but then it denies them the use of the best possible weapons. Yevon infuses the population with the humility that teaches them that they are powerless to defeat Sin themselves; instead, they must put their faith in the martyrs, the Summoners.

The Maester's Lie

As it turns out, Yevon has been preaching that faith in the teachings has the potential to eliminate Sin forever, but it knows that this is false. The subservience of the population, their piety, and their austere living have been in vain. According to

Yunalesca, Sin is eternal, and it is doubtful that humanity will ever be able to attain the purity necessary for the eradication of Sin. Yevon is based on a lie.

The deception runs deeper than the absence of a Promised Land. A duty of the Summoner is to send the dead to the Farplane, the place where the spirits of the dead reside. If this task is not accomplished, then it is possible that the spirits that remain will become Fiends and terrorize the living. Although the task is extremely important, it is not carried out. Rather, it is revealed that the ruling council of Maesters contains the unsent; even the supreme Maester Kinoc is unsent. Auron remarks in the temple at Bevelle, "So this is Yevon's true face, they betray their own teachings."

This revelation proves devastating to Yuna and Wakka. Lulu remains resolved until the confrontation with Yunalesca, where she is informed that the religion is useless in defeating Sin. If it is all a lie, does it mean that everything we have said so far is worthless? Not necessarily. Machiavelli, for instance, did not concern himself with the veracity of religion. When the Dominican friar Savonarola tried to establish a theocracy in his Florence, Machiavelli lauded his accomplishments. Still, he criticized the monk for trusting in otherworldly powers to protect him, rather than forming his own standing army. Thus, when Savonarola became a nuisance to the papacy and Alexander VI branded him a heretic and sent troops to arrest him on trumped-up charges, Savonarola was defenseless.

Machiavelli believed that religion can serve a political purpose, as well as a spiritual one. As he recalled in *The Discourses*, "Numa, finding the people ferocious and desiring to reduce them to civic obedience by means of the arts of peace, turned to religion as the instrument necessary above all others for the maintenance of a civilized state."[8] Ultimately, it does not matter whether a particular religion is true, but rather whether the people *believe* it to be true.

The Romans, Machiavelli noted, made extensive use of religion in motivating the population to civic loyalty. Consider how Scipio Africanus handled Hannibal's invasion. The people of Rome felt that the city was lost and began to abandon it. Scipio, seeing that there was still hope, forced the Roman citizens to swear an oath that they would stay and defend it. In doing so, the Roman Republic held together, eventually defeating Hannibal and razing the city of Carthage. The religiosity of the Romans was such that the people were more afraid of breaking their word than they were of transgressing the law.[9] Although we know little of the development of the Yevon theocracy, we do know that it unites all of the people of Spira, despite their differences in race (Guado, human, Ronso), attitude, and culture. Uniting the people under the banner of Yevon was more effective than any laws or use of force could have been.

As a political tool, religion is one of the most effective instruments in instituting and maintaining social order. The Romans were not concerned with whether the law of Rome made it illegal for them to flee, but once they swore an oath to their gods, they were compelled to stay. In the beginning of the game, Tidus asks what the penalties are if Yuna violates the teachings. The response is that "she could be excommunicated." For religious people, excommunication is a punishment without peer. Not only would being excommunicated deny Yuna the ability to make the pilgrimage, placing the responsibility for Sin's continued existence squarely on her, but she would also be shunned from Spiran society. As an outcast, her only recourse would be to join the heretical Al Bhed. Yuna might be strong enough to join the heretics, but the average Spiran wouldn't be—the principles have been so ingrained into their way of life that even as pariahs, they would still be compelled to follow the principles seeking forgiveness. Yevon binds Spira in a way that nothing else could. For Machiavelli, this was one of the most important aspects of religion, and although other methods can serve the same purpose, none of them are as effective as religion.

The End of Yevon

"For today little people lord it: they preach surrender and resignation and prudence and industry and consideration and the long etcetera of the small virtues."[10] Thus speaks Nietzsche's wandering prophet Zarathustra. The small virtues of humility and patience rule over our world, while in Spira the religion preaches an intellectual and technological limit. But for what purpose? We know that Yevon has lied to Spira: the Spirans have been promised that through piety, devotion, and their faith in the Summoners, the threat of Sin, their perpetual fear, will be vanquished. We know that in the end, it would have meant nothing. Yevon can stop Sin for only a short while; it inevitably returns, and all the while the people of Spira are kept in fear, unable and unwilling to fight on their own.

The only people whom Yevon sanctifies in Spira are the Summoners who have sacrificed themselves to rid the world of Sin. It is only in death that a person can achieve any kind of glory. The suffering of the living is only temporary, and death is the only true release from the miseries of the world. And so individuals do not seek to better themselves in the here and now, but instead they suffer the existence of Sin and tolerate the oppressiveness of a religion that violates its own precepts.

Is the solution the abolition of Yevon? The answer isn't so easy, and here Machiavelli and Nietzsche would disagree. By the end of the story, Yevon cannot possibly remain. Its very power in harnessing "the original and basic feeling [fear] of man" is no longer applicable.[11] The central aspect of life that kept the religious of Spira faithful has been destroyed. For so long the people have lived in fear of the monster, and without it their fate will be unknown. Nietzsche would see this fate as an opportunity for the people to move forward, transcending a life of service and humility, beginning instead to live for themselves, following their will, achieving worldly glory.

As a political philosopher, Machiavelli would fear for the people of Spira because the religion that united them is now irrelevant. The outcome of this could be a state of chaos, with factions rising against one another, perhaps resulting in the same type of war that caused the creation of Sin in the first place. The security of the people could be in grave jeopardy. Looking past that fact, Machiavelli would accept that the fetters of religion have now been broken. Either a new, compelling, and useful religion has to be found, or the new leaders would have to be quite exemplary in order to rule a people who no longer have a religion to unite them. In that case, theories regarding the conduct of rulers and government, like Machiavelli's, may find a new popularity.

Concerning the rest of us, whose sin is an internal idea, rather than a creature that swims in the sea, our two philosophers would have similar prescriptions. We must live our own lives now, rather than in fear or hope of the next life. So long as we concentrate on being humble, meek, and lowly, this life will pass us by. The principles and ideas that we must value in this life should be the ones that favor ourselves.[12]

NOTES

1. This *Art of War* is not to be confused with the Chinese general Sun Tzu's book of the same name.

2. Niccolò Machiavelli, *The Prince*, translated by W. K. Marriot (New York: Everyman Library, 1992), p. 70.

3. This theory also makes up a major theme in Machiavelli's *Art of War*.

4. Friedrich Nietzsche, "On the Genealogy of Morals," in *The Basic Writings of Nietzsche*, translated by Walter Kaufmann (New York: Modern Library, 2000), p. 473.

5. Nietzsche, "On the Genealogy of Morals," p. 476.

6. Friedrich Nietzsche, "Ecce Homo," in *The Basic Writings of Nietzsche*, translated by Walter Kaufmann (New York: Modern Library, 2000), p. 768.

7. Nietzsche, "On the Genealogy of Morals," p. 481.

8. Niccolò Machiavelli, *The Discourses on the First Decade of Titus Livy*, translated by Leslie J. Walker (New York: Penguin Books, 1973), p. 139.

9. Ibid., p. 140.

10. Friedrich Nietzsche, *Thus Spoke Zarathustra*, translated by Walter Kaufmann (New York: Penguin Books, 1969), p. 287.

11. Ibid., p. 302.

12. Special thanks to Alice Canaday and Laura Wysocki for comments and recommendations, as well as Ann Awad for the dialogue notes.

PART FIVE

OTHER WAYS TO ENJOY THE GAME SO IT NEVER ENDS

HUMAN, ALL TOO HUMAN: CLOUD'S EXISTENTIAL QUEST FOR AUTHENTICITY

Christopher R. Wood

Final Fantasy VII demarcates a rather peculiar place within the historical development of the *Final Fantasy* series. Putting aside the technological capabilities of the then new PlayStation console, *Final Fantasy VII* is known for leaving the first-time gamer with an experience that is nothing short of profound. The game's complex plot and intertwining side stories culminate in an adventure as entertaining as it is epic, with a lush and diverse world for us to explore at our own pace and by our own will. And while this world, with its high technologies and physics-defying magic, is surely nothing short of fantasy, in the end, the gamer is presented with an experience that, in many ways, mirrors that of our own experience in the not-so-fantastic real world.

Much of this is due to the memorable mannerisms of the game's primary characters. As we play through each of the game's three discs, we encounter a number of colorful person-alities whose hopes, fears, goals, and desires, however diverse, are revealed to be like our own. From an innocent and seem-ingly simple flower girl living in the slums of a harsh and desolate super-city, to a short-tempered and headstrong man with undying aspirations to become an astronaut, there is nothing tremendously unbelievable about the game's main characters that might prevent us from relating to them on a deep and sympathetic level. All of the game's playable charac-ters are accompanied by a rich backstory that not only explains their involvement contra the malevolent Shinra corporation but, more important, helps to drive their actions and aspira-tions just that much closer to home and into the hearts of the game's players.

Cloud Strife, *Final Fantasy VII*'s main protagonist, however, comes to us as somewhat more of a mystery. Passive and detached, Cloud tends to speak only when spoken to and rarely offers us anything beyond a series of short, arrogant remarks. Even well into the game's first disc, we're told very little about Cloud's history (other than his vague childhood ties to Tifa Lockheart and his self-proclaimed status as an "ex-SOLDIER"), and as the game's story progresses, much of what we learn about him tends to confuse, rather than illuminate. Heck, at times we even have reason to believe that the Cloud we *think* we know may be nothing other than a laboratory-grown cre-ation of the crazed Professor Hojo—a supposition that might help us justify his cold and apathetic attitude. Putting aside the mysteries surrounding Cloud's inception, however, there are ample reasons to argue that the Cloud we come to know is, in the end, really no different from you or me. Indeed, the German philosopher Friedrich Nietzsche (1844–1900) would likely agree that Cloud is, perhaps above every other charac-ter in the game, *all too human*. Cloud's struggle to overcome personal crisis can be interpreted along Nietzschean lines as nothing less than a true expression of the human spirit.

From the Midgar Train to the World at Large: Thrown into Existence

Existentialist philosophers such as Martin Heidegger (1889–1976), Jean-Paul Sartre (1905–1980), and the aforementioned Friedrich Nietzsche concerned themselves with the trials and tribulations of the everyday existing human individual.[1] Although not all existentialist philosophers share the same views regarding the nature of the human being, most of them agree on a number of undeniable facts of existence common to all individuals.

First and foremost, our initial births into the world are never of our choosing. We are, as Heidegger said so eloquently, "thrown" into the world with virtually no guidance as to what we should be doing, let alone who we are or what we should strive to become. Just as Cloud is thrown off Midgar's train into his first mission at Mako Reactor No. 1, we, too, are thrust into the world of existence without warning. This "thrownness," as scary as it may sound, is nevertheless a fundamental part of our very *being*: we cannot help but find ourselves submerged in a complex world with others, and, try as we may, the world is never something from which we can ever escape (astronaut jokes aside).

To be sure, as Heidegger argued, our connection to the world is not merely a simple relationship between a subject and an object (that is, between myself as a *person* to some*thing* out there that exists separately from me), but, rather, the world is a complex series of meanings that we find ourselves *in* at all times. To speak of the human being without reference to his or her world, then, is essentially to commit the error of trying to understand the human individual without looking at what it even means to *be* human in the first place. It is for this very reason that Heidegger often characterized being human as *being-in-the-world* and why a distinct understanding of this very intimate connection between the individual and his or her world provides one of the keys to living an authentic life.

It should go without saying that the "world" of *Final Fantasy VII* holds supreme value to most of the primary characters of the game. The core members of AVALANCHE, in particular, hold their planet in high regard as the very platform of existence. Indeed, the early missions to destroy Midgar's eight Mako reactors are carried out on the premise of not only saving human lives, but of saving *all* life in general. For Heidegger, however, the term *world* was not necessarily synonymous with the "planet" of *Final Fantasy VII*. *Planet*, as we come to learn through Bugenhagen's "Study of Planet Life," signifies a distinct living entity with its own life force; a sort of cosmic life that supports and produces all terrestrial lives. To Heidegger, the term *world* is of much more general import, understood primarily "as that '*wherein*' a factical [human being] as such can be said to 'live.' "[2] This distinction, though, has little bearing on the deep connection between the characters of *Final Fantasy VII* and their planet, as the death of the latter will most certainly bring about the end of the former.

Our earliest in-game experiences with Cloud reveal, however, that the intimate relationship between himself and the world is ultimately of little importance to him:

> Barret: Little by little the reactors'll drain out all the life. And that'll be that.
>
> Cloud: It's not my problem.
>
> Barret: The planet's dyin', Cloud!
>
> Cloud: The only thing I care about is finishin' this job before security and the Roboguards come.

And later:

> Tifa: The planet's dying. Slowly but surely it's dying. Someone has to do something.

Cloud: So let Barret and his buddies do something about it. It's got nothing to do with me.

It is clear that Cloud's own connection to the world—indeed, his own connection to the planet as such—is being ignored completely. His only concern, it would seem, is to be duly paid for his contributions to AVALANCHE's bombing missions. Although one might be tempted to ask what value his money might hold in a world without life, it is nevertheless obvious that Cloud is, at least initially, in complete denial of his own existence as *being-in-the-world*. But how did Cloud come to such a position? Is he justified in holding such a view? Perhaps more important, can his view *change*?

Is God Dead? Nietzschean Nihilism and Mako Morality

Our initial experience of being "thrown" into the world at birth is by no means the only cold fact of human existence. Most existentialist philosophers also assert that the human world is, by and large, a *godless* one and that the human individual is ultimately alone in the universe. Nietzsche, in particular, is famous for his proclamation that *God is dead* and that it just may be time to elect a new leader:

> God is dead. God remains dead. And we have killed him. How shall we, the murderers of all murderers, comfort ourselves? What was holiest and most powerful of all that the world has yet owned has bled to death under our knives. Who will wipe this blood off us? What water is there for us to clean ourselves? What festivals of atonement, what sacred games shall we have to invent? Is not the greatness of this deed too great for us? Must not we ourselves become gods simply to seem worthy of it?[3]

The passage above is arguably also one of Nietzsche's most misunderstood. Nietzsche is *not*, for one, claiming that God once *lived* in any sort of physical sense, only to have been somehow killed off by his followers. Rather, he is asserting that God has become *obsolete* and should no longer be recognized as providing us with any sort of real guidance in the modern world.

The importance of Nietzsche's proclamation is manifold. First off, it forces individuals to come to terms with their own deep-seated reliance on values that are not of their own making. This abrupt recognition, Nietzsche thought, would assuredly lead mankind into a state of *nihilism*, that is, the belief that no objective values are possible and that life as we know it is essentially devoid of meaning. After all, if God is the creator of all values and God is dead, then the foundations of our current values are revealed to be mistaken at best or completely arbitrary and groundless at worst. The crisis of nihilism, however, is not entirely negative for Nietzsche. In fact, it is only through our acceptance of God's absence that the individual can finally become liberated and learn to create values that are truly his or her own: for so long as we're looking toward an *otherworldly* God for the solution to our earthly problems, we're turning away from our *worldly* problems as such. That being said, the death of God ultimately signifies the opportunity for the human individual to re-fulfill the role of God by taking full control over his or her own domain and creating new values that are purely our own. Of course, one must also be continually aware of attempts made by others to create a new and equally false God from the rubble of the old—or, as in the case of Sephiroth, of attempting to achieve godhood itself!

The notion of the death of God and its accompanying state of nihilism is prevalent throughout *Final Fantasy VII*. The game's opening cinematic itself is notable in this regard for portraying a vast and starry sky sharply contrasted against the hustle and bustle of the streets of Midgar. Through the loud noise of the city, a quiet Aeris Gainsborough emerges from an alleyway, and despite her vivid surroundings, we can't help but think of her as being alone in the world. Indeed, her world is one of *nihilism*. Crime and desolation run rampant in the heart of the city, and very few seem willing to ponder whether a better lifestyle exists, choosing instead to live out their dreary lives much like common cattle confined to their own Mako-powered cages. As Jessie explains shortly after the first mission at the No. 1 Reactor,

> The 8 Reactors provide Midgar with electricity. Each town used to have a name, but no one in Midgar remembers them. Instead of names, we refer to them by numbered sectors. That's the kind of place this is.

Even Cloud, in what proves to be a rare display of empathy, agrees that Midgar presents us with "pretty unsettling scenery" and, given what we ourselves see throughout disc 1, it's difficult to disagree.

Jessie and the other members of Barret's ecoterrorist organization, AVALANCHE, however, are determined to provide the city—indeed, the world as a whole—with a solution to the growing problem of their modern Mako-powered nihilism. By destroying the world's Mako reactors, AVALANCHE hopes to liberate humanity from its dependence on the new "god" of Mako energy and force people to recognize their own value as the inhabitants of a thriving (not to mention *endangered*) world. Arguably, Barret and company are calling for the revaluation of values proposed by Nietzsche and the rebirth of a society founded on self-created values, not on values that have been forced on us by the oppressive powers of the Shinra corporation. Of course, the liberation of mankind and the creation of new values cannot happen solely through the actions of a select few: all people must come to recognize their own capacity for change, indeed, their own capacity for *freedom*.

Condemned to Be Free?

More so than any other existentialist, Jean-Paul Sartre high-lighted the paradoxical nature of human freedom. Indeed, most of Sartre's existential works can (and should) be read as descriptions of the effects that absolute freedom might have on the concretely existing human individual. Like Nietzsche, Sartre believed that the individual is born into a world free from the reins of God and that we, as human beings, are ultimately left to our own devices not only in creating values for ourselves, but also in determining what we truly are. For Sartre, this condition was best summarized by the statement "existence precedes essence." Unlike common household items or tools that are created by us in order to fulfill a specific role or purpose, human beings are peculiar insofar as they come into existence without any such predetermined essence or reason for being. We can easily conceive of the essence of Cloud's Buster Sword, for example, as an object used to inflict damage on enemies, but when it comes to defining the essence of Cloud *himself*, the question becomes considerably more difficult for us to answer. Is he a former inhabitant of Nibelheim? A childhood friend of Tifa? An ex-SOLDIER? A member of AVALANCHE? A sworn enemy of Sephiroth? An impersonator of Zack?

While Sartre considered our inherent lack of an essence to be liberating, insofar as it opens up an infinite number of possibilities for us, he also recognized that such a condition can be largely *unsettling*. The Buster Sword, whose essence is determined in advance of its creation, for example, need not worry about what it is in fact. Indeed, the Buster Sword is just that, *a sword*, and it will always *be* a sword until it no longer functions as such. The human individual, however, has no determinate essence and must choose what he or she will become. We may, one day, choose to become a member of SOLDIER, as Cloud did in his childhood, or, just as well, we may choose to become a member of AVALANCHE and fight against the malevolent

Shinra corporation instead. In either case, what we become is determined purely by the choices that we make and by how we project ourselves toward our own freely chosen goals. The catch, of course, is that our freedom is *absolute*: we cannot escape the fact that we *must* make our own choices, nor can we have anyone choose for us in our place—even choosing *not* to choose is a choice in itself!

As one might imagine, this absolute freedom can be quite cumbersome at times. So long as we are living in a world without a God-determined essence, we have no choice but to act according to our own free will—and by our own free will *alone*. Because of this, we are to be held completely responsible for our own actions, no exceptions. If we perform an act that we later decide to be reprehensible, such as the destruction of an entire sector of Midgar, citizens included, we have nobody to blame for it but ourselves. In such a case, I could not truthfully say that God created me in order to perform such a terrible act, because, as a free being whose existence precedes his essence, I am always free to choose otherwise (namely, to refuse to carry out the destructive act). Cloud is, of course, no exception to the rule. He must, at nearly every turn, choose which course of action to take, and we, as the game's players, must guide him along the way. In encountering Aeris for the first time, for example, we can choose to address or ignore her concerns. Similarly, we can choose to buy a flower from her or instead tell her to "forget it." We cannot, however, avoid making these choices altogether. In fact, as we come to learn later on, the choices we do make will, in part, determine how we are perceived by others. If we choose to treat Aeris poorly, we should not be surprised if she does not show up as Cloud's late-night date at the Gold Saucer in disc 1.[4] Of course, while there are times in which we might want to escape the consequences of our choices, it would appear that, in reality, it is not possible for us to do so. Indeed, we are, as Sartre himself would say, *condemned to be free* and must, as a result, accept the responsibility that accompanies our absolute freedom.

The *Bad Faith* of SOLDIER

Although it is true that the human individual is necessarily free, Sartre contended that we often attempt to deny our own freedom through various means. We might, for example, pretend that we are people whose jobs or roles within society completely determine the choices we make and that, as a result, we could *not* choose otherwise. A weapon salesman, for example, might excuse his cowardice in times of war on the grounds that he is *merely* a salesman and that it's not in his "salesman nature" to participate in acts of combat. Of course, in reality, the salesman isn't *only* just that: he could, at any time, choose to arm himself with his own wares and fend off the waves of incoming monsters—whether he would be *wise* to do so is, of course, another matter altogether!

What's interesting to note about these personal cover-ups, however, is that we as human beings have the peculiar capacity to actually *believe* them ourselves. Unlike blatant lies in which the liar fully understands that he is being dishonest, acts of *self-deception*, Sartre contended, call for the liar to dupe himself. Sartre explained the phenomenon by describing the motions of a particular waiter in a café:

> Let us consider this waiter in the café. His movement is quick and forward, a little too precise, a little too rapid. He comes toward the patrons with a step a little too quick. He bends forward a little too eagerly; his voice, his eyes express an interest a little too solicitous for the order of the customer. . . . He is playing, he is amusing himself. But what is he playing? We need not watch long before we can explain it: he is playing at *being* a waiter in a café.[5]

The key word here really is *being*. The waiter's rigid movements are not merely an attempt at imitating the characteristics that one might find present in a perfect waiter.

More fundamentally, his attempt is that of passing himself off completely as some*thing* that he is not. To be sure, the waiter is not merely a waiter: he certainly has a life outside of the café, complete with his own hobbies, interests, and desires (at least, we would hope!). Nevertheless, he has chosen to portray himself as some sort of waiterlike "robot" by ignoring everything that's irrelevant to being a waiter and adopting instead a series of actions that are clearly not natural to him. But worst of all, he believes that he can actually pull it off! This belief, that it might be possible for us to sever our ties with our freedom and act as if we are not actually responsible for our own actions, is called *bad faith* and was considered by Sartre to be a mode of inauthentic being that is all too common in each of our lives, the lives of *Final Fantasy VII* being no exception.

Consider the case of Cloud. In his initial appearances, he portrays himself as a cold and arrogant mercenary whose only care is to be reimbursed for his contributions to AVALANCHE. His responses to others are short and to the point, and he has no apparent desire go beyond what is strictly required of him. His oversized Buster Sword, perhaps a bit too large for his comparatively small frame, is displayed with pride, and his uniform, while matching that of his enemy, is worn without shame. When asked for his opinion or in times when others might express theirs, he is quick to disclose that such matters are insignificant to him and that the only matter of relevance is that hefty sum of gil at the end of the day. But what can we say to this? Well, to Sartre, the answer is clear: Cloud is playing at *being* a SOLDIER!

Inauthenticity and the Life of the Mercenary

Existentialist philosophers such as Sartre, Heidegger, and Nietzsche would all agree that not only is the human life solely what we make of it, but that what we make of it can be determined only by our own free choices and actions. They also tend to agree that the choices we do make will inevitably lead us down one of two possible paths in life: the *authentic* path, marked by the acceptance of the factical conditions of existence and the will to perpetually create new values, and the *inauthentic* path, marked by the denial of human freedom and the adherence to faulty or stagnant values. Authentic individuals thus possess a strong degree of self-mastery and creativity, whereas inauthentic individuals wallow in slavishness, seeking largely to relieve themselves of the weight of their own responsibilities.

The evolution of Cloud's story is of particular interest in this regard, as the choices that Cloud makes would seem to carry him from one extreme to the other. Indeed, one might even go so far as to say that Cloud's "quest" in *Final Fantasy VII* is not so much one to save the world, but rather to come to terms with the coherence of his own role within it. To begin, in his earliest incarnations (shown to us in the Lifestream flashbacks after the destruction of Mideel in disc 2), we find a young Cloud yearning for attention and acceptance in the world:

> Cloud: I really wanted to play with everyone, but was never allowed into the group.

Then later:

> Cloud: I began to think I was different. . . . That I was different from those immature kids. That then . . . may be . . . just maybe, they would invite me in. I thought that might happen, so I hung around. . . . I was so prejudiced. And . . . weak.

Of course, as we know, Cloud never won acceptance into Tifa's childhood gang. The open possibilities of the world, however, would soon provide him with new opportunities to prove to Tifa that perhaps he is not as weak as the others think:

> Cloud: Come this spring . . . I'm leaving this town for Midgar.

Tifa: . . . All boys are leaving our town.

Cloud: But I'm different from all of them. I'm not just going to find a job. . . . I want to join SOLDIER. I'm going to be the best there is, just like Sephiroth.

While Cloud's boyhood dream could perhaps be passed off as just that, his decision to pursue a career in SOLDIER would certainly prove to be life-changing. One might even liken this event to the Nietzschean death of God for Cloud, insofar as it marks the adoption of a radical new set of values. Indeed, in these latter stages of his childhood, Cloud comes to the realization that the values of his youth that have been bestowed on him by his community have essentially become obsolete: his attempts to fit in with his peers by "being himself" have failed, and he finds himself left only to his own devices and the breadth of the open world. The decision to climb the ranks to SOLDIERhood would seem to offer the potential solution to his growing nihilism, but in that same decision also lurks the danger of growing further away from his goal of true independence.

Unfortunately, Cloud's choice seems only to have led him down the latter path. In the first half of the game, Cloud comports himself wholly as if he succeeded in rising up to the top rank of First Class SOLDIER. Even his own memories (as disclosed to us in the early flashback scene at Kalm in disc 1) portray him as having fought side by side with Sephiroth against the dangerous monsters of Mount Nibel. What we learn in the second half, however, is a completely different story: Cloud never became a First Class SOLDIER. In fact, Cloud never joined SOLDIER at all. As we learn in the Lifestream flashback scenes in disc 2, his service to Shinra's military forces never went beyond that of a common guard:

Cloud: I . . . never made it as a member of SOLDIER. I even left my hometown telling everyone I was going to join, but . . . I was so embarrassed. . . . I didn't want to see anybody.

And by this, the truth is revealed: Cloud's initial "tough guy" attitude of the game's first half was never of his own making but rather was adopted entirely through his own conception of what a First Class SOLDIER should *be*. In the optional Shinra mansion flashback sequence of disc 3, we learn that Cloud's idea to work as a mercenary in Midgar, as well as his SOLDIER uniform and characteristic Buster Sword, all belonged to Zack, Aeris's then boyfriend and a true First Class SOLDIER:

> Zack: Listen, I'm gonna become a mercenary and that's that. Boring stuff, dangerous stuff, anything for money. I'm gonna be rich! . . . Cloud? What are YOU gonna do?

Having just escaped his Mako containment chamber in the mansion's basement laboratory and seemingly unable (or unwilling) to respond, Cloud remains silent in contrast to Zack's excitement, leaving Zack to choose his future for him:

> Zack: Mercenaries, Cloud. That's what you an' me are gonna be.

As we soon find out, however, Zack never gets to live out his dream and is quickly shot down by Shinra guards on his arrival at Midgar. Cloud, however, appearing in a near-dead state, survives the onslaught unscathed, and, after waking up from the events that just transpired, he claims Zack's sword, as well as Zack's dream of a mercenary life, as his own.

From SOLDIER to Savior: Cloud's Turn to Authenticity

The Cloud of the game's first half is, without doubt, a Cloud living in *bad faith*. His choice to leave Nibelheim was a choice made on the grounds of trying to become some*thing* that he is not, namely, a person of great strength who is respected for his high-standing status among Shinra's military elite. Of course, the Cloud we eventually come to know possesses neither of these two features. He is merely an ordinary person seeking his own path in the world, perhaps no different in this regard from you or me. Unfortunately, rather than abiding by his own free will and working to create his *own* values, Cloud chooses instead to take the inauthentic route and adopt a persona that is already well established—a persona that he believes will readily propel him into a position of respect and admiration. These mistakes, however, are not entirely unrecoverable. Cloud, as a free human being, is endowed with the capacity to choose otherwise and, more specifically, to make the choice to change his ways. And although we may have reason to believe that Cloud's exposure to Mako radiation is detrimental to his ability to function autonomously, his willingness to face the darkness of his past at the start of the second half of the game is a strong indication of his desire to start anew, indeed, to start life *authentically*.

After Tifa and Cloud wake up from their submergence in the Lifestream after the attacks on Mideel in disc 2, Tifa finds herself, by whatever means, capable of entering Cloud's mind and following him through the depths of his own memories. Together, they revisit the fateful mission at Mount Nibel as it frequently appears in the game's earlier scenes. It is here that Cloud, by his own will, is able to come to terms with the inauthenticity of his past and ultimately give new meaning to his future. We learn, first off, that Cloud's boyhood weakness and desire to impress Tifa were indeed his primary reasons for pursuing a career with SOLDIER:

> Cloud: I was so angry. . . . Angry at myself for my weakness. . . . That was the first time I heard about

Sephiroth. If I got strong like Sephiroth, then everyone might . . . If I could just get stronger . . . then even Tifa would have to notice me.

Second, in the same episode, we affirm that Cloud never did partake in the Mount Nibel mission as a SOLDIER. Instead, he found himself so embarrassed by his own lies of SOLDIERdom that he chose to hide his face from his hometown by wearing his uncomfortable guard's mask for the duration of the mission. Third, and perhaps most important, we learn that although he considered himself weak and cowardly, it was Cloud and *not* Zack who mustered up the strength and courage necessary to put a stop to Sephiroth by throwing him into the Mako reactor at Mount Nibel, effectively preventing (or at least delaying) his terrible spree to destroy the planet.

Indeed, although Cloud had hitherto lived his life in an inauthentic state of perpetual *bad faith*, after coming to terms with his own failures (as well as realizing his own strength as a free individual fully capable of vanquishing the powerful Sephiroth), Cloud awakens from his stupor and returns to his friends with new hope. At this point, the Cloud we encounter appears wholly transformed:

Cloud: I never was in SOLDIER. I made up the stories about what happened to me five years ago, about being in SOLDIER. I left my village looking for glory, but never made it in to SOLDIER. . . . I was so ashamed of being so weak; then I heard this story from my friend Zack. . . . And I created an illusion of myself made up of what I had seen in my life. . . . And I continued to play the charade as if it were true.

Barret: Illusion, huh . . . ? Pretty damn strong for a 'lusion, I'd say.

This noble admittance to having chosen the inauthentic path of life is soon followed by the decision to live life to its fullest, with all of its hiccups and flaws:

> Cloud: . . . I'm . . . Cloud . . . the master of my own illusionary world. But I can't remain trapped in an illusion any more. . . . I'm going to live my life without pretending.

With that, Cloud vows to carry onward with AVALANCHE's original mission to protect the planet at all costs and to defeat Sephiroth once and for all. For it is at this point that he has come to the realization that the world is indeed an integral part of his very being and that regardless of his futile attempts to deny the conditions of his existence, he will always be fully responsible for his own actions and, consequently, the true master of his own destiny.

Cloud's Choice and Ours

As we have seen, the story of *Final Fantasy VII* is wrought with numerous existentialist themes. As players of the game, we find ourselves thrown into a godless world of modern nihilism and must, through no avenue other than our free choices (and, of course, with our controllers in hand), come to terms with our place within it, our relationships with others and, perhaps most important, with ourselves. Through the perspective of Cloud Strife, in particular, we experience a wide array of life choices and address their consequences with a depth of character that is not typical of other games. Indeed, the choices that Cloud makes not only illustrate the breadth of the human spirit but also demonstrate our capability as individuals to actualize our potential through the realization of our own freedom and responsibilities. And while these realizations ultimately enable Cloud to save the planet from its gravest dangers, they also afford him the opportunity to complete the most fundamental quest of all: to live life *authentically*.

NOTES

1. Particularly observant players of *Final Fantasy VII* might recall that the name "Heidegger" is also shared by the head of Shinra's public safety maintenance department. There is little reason to believe, however, in any significant connection between the two.

2. Martin Heidegger, *Being and Time*, translated by John Macquarrie and Edward Robinson (New York: Harper & Row, 1962), p. 93.

3. Friedrich Nietzsche, *The Gay Science*, in Walter Kaufmann, ed., *The Portable Nietzsche* (New York: Penguin, 1982), p. 95.

4. The female character who accompanies Cloud for this particular event is determined by (a) how the player responds to dialogue with those characters, and (b) how often and when that character is placed in the same party with Cloud. If all female characters are treated especially poorly and/or neglected by the player, Barret will show up for the "date" instead.

5. Jean-Paul Sartre, *Being and Nothingness*, translated by Hazel Barnes (New York: Washington Square Press, 1992), pp. 101–102.

IS THE FEAR OF
STOPPING JUSTIFIED?

Kevin Fitzpatrick

Mr. 288 told me that I understand what it means to
live and to die. . . . But it's only because I thought
stopping was different from dying . . . I don't think
I really understand what it means to live and to die.
Where do we come from . . . ? Do we go back there
when we die . . . ? If that's what it means to live . . .
I wonder where I came from . . . ? Where will I end
up when I die? Why am I shaking? What is this that
I'm feeling . . . ?

—Vivi Orunitia, *Final Fantasy IX*

In *Final Fantasy IX*, Vivi Orunitia is a precocious nine-year-old
whose nature and origin are as mysterious to him as they are to us.
He begins to overtly quest for answers about what he is and the
circumstances of his "birth" after he encounters a factory that
is manufacturing "dolls" that bear a striking resemblance to
him. As the story reveals the mysteries of his nature, we find
out that he is the prototype creation of a man named Kuja,

who created Vivi through a strange amalgamation of souls and black magic.

The factory Vivi encounters is creating more of his kind, an artificial race referred to as "Black Mages." Most of the Black Mages lack self-awareness and are controlled as puppets. Some Black Mages attain awareness over time, however, and escape their controller's influence.

When Vivi happens upon a village of Black Mage escapees, he begins to consider his own demise. The following conversation takes place in a newly formed cemetery where Black Mages have begun to bury those who have stopped moving:

> Black Mage No. 56: I . . . I came here with Mr. 36. We escaped together. We had so many things to learn. It was really scary at first, but we helped each other. Then one day, Mr. 36 stopped moving. He just stopped . . . wouldn't move or say anything. My friend who knows lots of things told me this was what 'death' was, and we had to bury him. Mr. 36 is buried under the ground now. But I don't understand why. He's going to come out again one day, right? When he does, I'm going to wash him off in the pond.
>
> Vivi: Wh-What's he talking about . . . ?
>
> Black Mage No. 288: . . .
>
> Vivi: Was it a disease? Or was he hurt?
>
> Black Mage No. 288: . . .
>
> Vivi: Tell me! Why?

In this scene we learn that Vivi doesn't understand why someone would die without being sick or injured, and the fact that he doesn't ask whether Mr. 36 was elderly also suggests that Vivi fails to consider aging as a cause of death.

We discover in later conversations between Vivi and Mr. 288 that Vivi and the Black Mages of the village fear death. But is their fear justified?

If the fear of death is justified, then we should be able to point to something that is lost through death. People can be harmed only if one or more of their values, and therefore their meaning or purpose for living, is in some way lost or hindered. Therefore, the extent to which death can be an impediment to the satisfaction of a person's values determines the extent to which it is justifiable for that person to fear death.

Stopping's Effect on Subjective Values: Morality, Knowledge, and the Value of Life

One of the more striking values that Vivi exhibits is morality. At various times, he refers to people as being "evil" and refers to specific acts as "bad." He not only wants to avoid being evil and bad, but he wants others not to view him as being evil or bad. Consider his reaction to being mistaken for the manipulated Black Mages that are terrorizing much of the world. Vivi emphatically remarks at such times that he would never hurt anyone. He would not hurt someone because he believes that it would be wrong; Vivi values morality.

Can the value of morality be hindered by death? If Vivi believes that being moral simply entails not doing evil acts, and he performs no evil acts, then it doesn't matter whether he dies today or a hundred years from now; he will be equally moral, regardless. If, however, Vivi has failed to live a moral life, then he might need time to be a good person in order to make up for the time that he spent being immoral. As the timeline increases, the percentage of his acts that are immoral would decrease. So if Vivi ever believed that he had been significantly immoral, then death could be considered a hindrance to his satisfaction of morality. Of course, living longer would also add more time to be tempted to be immoral. So perhaps if he has lived a moral life thus far, then death should be a welcomed event (from the point of view of morality). In addition to morality, Vivi also values knowledge. Questions about where he comes from, what he is, and whether he will die drive Vivi. With this value in mind, Vivi would be harmed less if he died later in the story than toward the beginning, simply because he would know more of the things that he desires to know.

Perhaps the most basic value anyone can have is the value of his or her own continued existence. Some people fear death because what they value most is who and what they are and the fact that they continue to exist; if they cease to exist, then all other values that they may possess cease to exist as well. Vivi appears to value specific people and life in general; this is why he takes part in fighting and defeating an entity named Necron, who is determined to destroy all life. If Necron is to be believed, then he is eternal and will always return to try to destroy life. Vivi's valuing of life in general could be hindered in its satisfaction by his death because he would no longer be around to protect it. So, if he does value protecting life in this manner, death will always be a harm to him. Does Vivi have this fear? It is hard to say. The storyline of *Final Fantasy IX* does address this fear, however, and provides a solution.

According to Garland, who is the man behind the curtain, in many respects, all memories that anyone experiences throughout his or her life are eternal. Concerning the true nature of memories, Garland says the following:

> Do not limit memory to just one individual's experiences from birth. That is only the surface. Every life born into this world, whether natural or artificial, requires a parent. And that parent also requires a parent. Life is connected, one to another. . . . If you trace the root of all life, there exists one source. The same can be said for memory. All life constitutes an intelligence

that holds memory beyond experience. Memory is not isolated within individuals. It is an accumulation of generations of memories that continues to evolve. You can say that memory and evolution go hand in hand. But most life-forms do not understand the true nature of memories . . . which explains why most memories never cross paths.

There are many ways that one can interpret this description of the nature of memories. I take it, however, that one point is explicit: as long as there is life, memories are eternal. Vivi's friend Zidane, whom Garland is addressing in the previous quotation, overcomes his own fear of death by believing that the important part of what we are as individuals is our memories, and that our memories will last eternally.

Vivi never comments on Garland's memory claims, and it is quite possible Vivi does not even hear what Garland says. But there is some connection between Garland's claims about the importance of memories and Vivi. According to Garland, memory and evolution both flow out of procreation. This may be why in the end it is suggested that Vivi might well have died, but that this is somehow okay. Vivi's descendants, who have a link through Vivi to the origin of life, may well carry his memories and the memories of everyone who is on the path from the origin of life to Vivi.

Whether or not Vivi's procreation is supposed to be linked to Garland's and Zidane's account of memories, many people find shelter from their fears about death by having children. The fact that Vivi may have chosen such shelter is suggested across two scenes. The first occurs when most of the citizens of the Black Mages' village willingly leave to aid Kuja. The Mages do not agree with what Kuja wants them to do, but they help him because he claims he will extend their lives if they help him in his pursuits. Two of the Mages, however, stay behind to look after a Chocobo egg. Apparently, they would rather make sure a new life is brought into the world than pursue a longer life for themselves. Vivi watches this scene curiously.

The second scene takes place at the story's conclusion when Vivi's children are present, but Vivi is nowhere to be found. Interestingly enough, the ending is clearly meant to be a happy ending, whether he is still alive or not. The similar mannerisms of Vivi's son and his recognition of people Vivi knew from stories Vivi had told him may well be an attempt to show that some important part of Vivi has been passed on to at least one of his children.

These are just some of the values that Vivi likely holds. But regardless of what Vivi's values or his thoughts about death truly are, it is death's impact on his value satisfaction that determines whether any harm is done to him by his death.

Necron a Hero?!

We need to consider whether some values are objectively valuable, and if so, what that means for the fear of death. By "objectively valuable," I mean that a value has an intrinsic worth independent of anyone actually valuing it, or at least independent of anyone believing that he or she values it, in the same way that the force of gravity exists whether we believe it does or not. If objective values exist, then these values must be considered when determining whether Vivi can be harmed by death, for an objective value would be important for Vivi regardless of his beliefs concerning the value.

The philosopher Epicurus (341–270 BCE) believed that the only thing that had objective value was happiness; he argued that death should not be feared. For Epicurus, happiness is a state that occurs from being without any physical or mental pain.[1] Therefore, in order for Vivi's happiness to be hindered, he must feel pain, either physically or mentally. But if he is dead, then he will be incapable of experiencing anything, including all forms of pain. Dying may be painful, but death itself is nothing. Vivi and the other Black Mages don't even need to fear the pain of dying, however. Stopping seems to be devoid of any pain; life simply ends.

The deaths of others sometimes hinder happiness. Vivi, for example, is saddened by Dagger's mourning the loss of her mother:

> I was really confused when my grandpa died. He told me, "Vivi, no need be sad." So I told myself, I can't be sad. That's why I felt confused again when I heard that everyone was stopping around him. I don't know what to do or what to feel. . . . But when I saw Dagger crying when her mom died, I wasn't confused anymore. I was sad.

In this scene, it is unclear exactly why Vivi feels sad. It could be that Vivi is sad simply because Dagger is upset, and Dagger is someone whose happiness Vivi values. Or, he might be sad because seeing Dagger's reaction gives Vivi license to feel the sadness over his grandfather's death. It could even be that Dagger's reaction toward her mother's death resonates with Vivi regarding his feelings toward the stopping of people in general. Perhaps he is mourning all of the deaths that he has witnessed and maybe even the deaths that he knows will come.

Regardless of why Vivi is sad in this scene, the death of another has reduced his own happiness, as well as Dagger's. If happiness can be decreased by the death of a loved one, then Vivi's fear of death could justifiably result from the knowledge that his death will likely cause unhappiness for those who love him. This justifiable fear, however, is the result of Vivi valuing people who love him or valuing happiness itself, as opposed to valuing his own happiness. As such, this shows only that valuing other people's happiness can lead to some justification for fearing death.

Epicurus believed that people like Vivi fear their own death because they believe that their own individual happiness will be hindered by death. This is a mistake, though, because death itself is completely innocuous.[2] Realizing that death in no way harms us, we can free ourselves from the pain caused by the fear of death.

Necron from *Final Fantasy IX* actually comes quite close to espousing Epicurus's philosophy. After Kuja destroys the crystal that is the source of all life, Necron says the following:

> I exist for one purpose . . . to return everything back to the zero world, where there is no life and no crystal to give life. In a world of nothing, fear does not exist. This is the world that all life desires. . . . Your fears have already deluded you. One day, you will choose destruction over existence, as Kuja did. When he sought to destroy the crystal, the purpose of life ended. Now, come. Enter the zero world that you desire.

From this statement, we can see that Necron believes that something in Kuja's act of destroying the source of life has ended the purpose of life. This means that Necron believed that there was purpose in living before Kuja's action. Necron also indicates that it was the fear of death that motivated Kuja's action. If the fear of death is the cause of the action that destroys the purpose of life in Necron's eyes, then the following claim is highly plausible: Necron believes, as Epicurus did, that happiness is an objective value of such importance that if it is not satisfied, then the purpose of life ends. He says as much:

> All life bears death from birth. Life fears death, but lives only to die. It starts with anxiety. Anxiety becomes fear. Fear leads to anger . . . anger leads to hate . . . hate leads to suffering. The only cure for this fear is total destruction. Kuja was a victim of his own fear. He concluded he could only save himself by destroying the origin of all things—the crystal.

So Necron believes people cannot escape the fear of death they feel. If Kuja's actions prove this, then Epicurus's theory of happiness accounts for why the fear of death destroys the purpose of life. This follows because if happiness is the source of all life's purpose, then no one can ever satisfy its purpose so long as he or she fears death.

Necron differs from Epicurus in thinking that people cannot remove the fear of death. If Epicurus had become convinced that people could not avoid the fear of death, then he may well have agreed with Necron that life should end because it lacks purpose. After all, Necron is attempting to do nothing more than remove all possible harm.

As for Epicurus's argument that harm cannot result from death, there are ways to oppose this argument. Perhaps the most promising attack on the Epicurean argument is to claim that people can be deprived of happiness or at least the potential for achieving happiness by death. To see the force of this position, all we have to do is think of things that make us happy in life that we will not be able to enjoy in death, such as love, yummy frogs, Chocobo hot and cold, and the festival of the hunt.

But the Epicurean presents a challenge to the defender of a deprivation argument: if death can harm us, then it must harm us at some time, but since we can only be harmed if we can experience pain, then when does death harm us?[3]

A Formula to an Answer

The question of whether death harms Vivi comes down to which values we attribute to him; what objective values, if any, we believe exist in *Final Fantasy IX*; and what is the state of value satisfaction these values possess relative to Vivi at the time that he stops. The scope of this chapter stops short of claiming what values are objective in the world of *Final Fantasy IX*, as well as of giving a definitive answer to the sum total and degree of values that Vivi holds. But, of course, none of this was really about Vivi anyway, was it? Ultimately, Vivi is just a vehicle for thinking about what you value and whether you should fear death. And in the end, only you can answer those questions.

NOTES

1. See Epicurus, *The Essential Epicurus*, translated by Eugene O'Connor (Amherst, NY: Prometheus Books, 1993).

2. See Dane R. Gordon and David B. Suits, *Epicurus: His Continuing Influence and Contemporary Relevance* (Rochester, NY: RIT Cary Graphic Arts Press, 2003).

3. See James Warren, *Facing Death: Epicurus and His Critics* (Oxford: Clarendon Press, 2004). Contemporary defenders of deprivation arguments differ in their stances with regard to the timing of death's harm. Some of the claimed times when harm occurs are at the moment of death (Julian Lamont), before death (Joel Feinberg and George Pitcher), throughout all eternity (Fred Feldman), and at no particular time (Thomas Nagel). The arguments for each of these would take far too much time to expound here, but their *existence* reveals the increasing complexity of the question of whether death can justifiably harm Vivi.

WHAT'S IN A NAME?
CID, CLOUD, AND HOW
NAMES REFER

Andrew Russo and Jason Southworth

Final Fantasy is one of the longest-running video game series of all time, and an interesting feature of these games is that the worlds in which they take place are rarely connected to one another. Despite the lack of coherence across *FF* games, some peculiar features may arouse curiosity from a longtime fan. For instance, the name "Cid" appears in many of the *FF* games. More paradoxical is the case of Cloud Strife, who appears to be the same individual, referred to by the same name, in different *FF* worlds—*FFVII* and *FF Tactics*. Intuitively, we think that the name "Cid" refers to a different individual in each *FF* world. The name "Cloud Strife," however, seems to refer to the same individual across the *FFVII* world and the *FF Tactics* world. Although most fans make these observations and move on, philosophers of language see an opportunity to begin a discussion of how names refer to certain objects in the world. Can the best theories of how names refer to various objects accommodate these intuitions concerning the names "Cid" and "Cloud Strife"?[1]

If Names Are Arbitrary, Is Cloud? The Direct Reference Theory

The simplest theory of the way names connect to things in the world is known as the direct reference theory. We call it "direct" because it takes for granted the relationship between the name and what it denotes. Simply put, according to the direct reference theory, names are just arbitrary *labels*. Much like *"Final Fantasy X"* written on a disc labels what game content is on the disc, names are labels for whatever falls in their extension. Due to such arbitrariness, there need not be any special relationship between, for example, two individuals with the name "Cid" or the name "Cloud Strife."

A flaw with the direct reference theory concerns identity statements. For instance, the protagonist of *FFVIII*, known as Squall Leonheart, appears in *Kingdom Hearts I* and *II* with the name "Leon." If these individuals are identical, then the following is a true statement: Squall = Leon. This identity statement contains two proper names, which pick out the same individual. If the direct reference theory of names is correct, then the identity statement is trivial—it gives us no new information. It merely states that this individual is identical to himself. This runs counter to our intuitions about identity, however, because the statement does seem to be informative. If a logical consequence of the direct reference theory of names is in conflict with our intuitions about certain identity statements, then maybe we should inquire into an account that attempts to square with these intuitions. Bertrand Russell (1872–1970) offered a descriptivist theory that endeavors to do just that.[2]

According to Russell's descriptivism, names are simply *abbreviations* for definite descriptions. A definite description is a description that applies to one and only one person or thing, while an indefinite description applies to more than one person or thing. The definite description associated with the name "Cloud Strife" might be:

(1) The Materia blade–wielding protagonist of *FFVII*.

This description does not fit anyone besides Cloud Strife, so it is definite, whereas the description "a protagonist of *FF*" could apply to several people in addition to Cloud Strife, such as Yuna and Tidus, and therefore is considered indefinite. Russell argued that the proper name "Cloud Strife" means the same thing as (1). Therefore, "Cloud Strife" is simply an abbreviation of (1). When someone says, "Cloud Strife just used Omnislash," we could replace that statement with "the Materia blade-wielding protagonist of *FFVII* just used Omnislash," with no loss of meaning.

To fully comprehend Russell's descriptivism, it is important to understand how Russell dealt with definite descriptions by themselves. He told us that appearances are deceptive when it comes to the "superficial structure" of definite descriptions. They appear to be very simple claims, when in fact they make a set of more complex ones. The complex set of claims results from the article "the" in the definite description. Consider the following:

(2) The Materia blade–wielding protagonist of *FFVII* is blond.

Here, we are attributing the property of blondness to the referent of (1), Cloud Strife. Statement number (2) hides the following set of claims:

(a) At least one person wields a Materia blade and is the protagonist of *FFVII*, *and*

(b) At most, one person wields a Materia blade and is the protagonist of *FFVII*, *and*

(c) Whoever wields a Materia blade and is the protagonist of *FFVII* is blond.

As Russell saw it, (a), (b), and (c) are necessary so long as (2) is true. If the Materia blade–wielding protagonist of *FFVII* is blond, then there must be at least one Materia blade–wielding protagonist. If there were more than one blond blade-wielding protagonist, then an indefinite description should have been used, for example: *a* Materia blade–wielding protagonist of *FFVII* is blond. So, there is at most one Materia blade–wielding protagonist. Finally, if the Materia blade–wielding protagonist is blond, then it follows that a claim stating such is true. Therefore, for Russell, names are simply abbreviations for a set of claims of the form of (a) through (c).[3]

So far, we have concentrated on the semantics of proper names, but what about Russell's theory of referring? How does Russell explain the fact that the name "Cloud Strife" refers to Cloud Strife instead of to someone else? Because the name "Cloud Strife" abbreviates the definite description in (1), then the referent of "Cloud Strife" is determined to be whatever satisfies (1). In other words, the referent of a proper name is whatever is described by the definite description of which the name is an abbreviation. Here is another example to make things clearer. Take the following definite description:

(3) The gunblade-wielding protagonist of *FFVIII*.

What is the name of the individual who satisfies (3)? It is "Squall Leonheart," and simply by satisfying (3), the individual Squall Leonheart is referred to by the name "Squall Leonheart."

Remember, the reason that we rejected the direct reference theory was that it was counterintuitive concerning identity statements such as "Squall = Leon," and Russell fares much better in this respect. This may not be obvious, so let's take it step by step. First, take the name "Squall" and (3), a definite description that offers the same semantic contribution as "Squall." Second, take the name "Leon" and a definite description that offers the same semantic contribution to it, something like:

(4) The man from Radiant Garden who helps guide Sora in the fight against the Heartless.

Because (3) and (4) offer the same semantic contribution to "Squall" and "Leon," respectively, we can form the unabbreviated identity statement as:

(5) The gunblade-wielding protagonist of *FFVIII* = the man from Radiant Garden who helps guide Sora in the fight against the Heartless.

By making explicit the logical reality behind the names "Squall" and "Leon," we can see how (5) is informative. The new information we learn is that the protagonist of *FFVIII*, who wields a gunblade, is also from Radiant Garden and helps Sora battle the Heartless. In this way, Russell's descriptivism offers both an intuitive account of the semantic contribution of names and a simple theory of how the referent of a name is determined.

What does Russell's descriptivism say about the relationship between the referents who share a proper name across the *FF* worlds? The name "Cid" would abbreviate different definite descriptions given the different games. In the world of *FFVII*, the name "Cid" would abbreviate "the pilot of the *Highwind*"; in *FFIX*, "the King of Lindblum"; in *FFX*, "the brother of Rikku"; and so on. Given that the name "'Cid'" is an abbreviation for these various definite descriptions in different *FF* worlds, and that the individuals who satisfy the definite descriptions in each world are different (for instance, the individual who is the King of Lindblum is not the same individual as the pilot of the *Highwind*), it follows that the referents who share the proper name "Cid" have no special relation to one another. This is good for Russell, as it conforms to our intuitions.

Interestingly, Zidane appears to be using Russell's descriptivism at one point in *FFIX*. Although it's a small moment in the game, most *FF* fans remember when, in a weapon shop, Zidane sees a sword that looks exactly like Cloud's Materia blade. Zidane says, "I remember a guy with spiky hair who carried something like this." This was a way of saying to the players of the game, "I remember Cloud Strife," and that is exactly how the audience took the utterance. "The guy with spiky hair who carried a Materia blade" is a definite description that is abbreviated by "Cloud Strife."

Would the Real Cloud Strife Please Wave His Blade?

One problem for Russell's descriptivism is that in the case of Cloud Strife, it does not come to a determinate conclusion. Depending on what definite description a speaker associates with the name "Cloud Strife," the referents of the name in *FFVII* and *FF Tactics* might or might not be identical. This indeterminacy is counterintuitive, because we think that surely we should be able to determine whether two referents who share a proper name are the same individual. In order to make this point explicit, let's associate the definite description

> (6) The Materia blade–wielding man with spiky blond hair

with the name "Cloud Strife." If (6) is so associated, then we can see that both the individual in *FFVII* and the individual in *FF Tactics* satisfy (6), hence making the referents identical.

If, instead, we use

> (7) The Materia blade–wielding man with the astrological sign Leo

we see that the individual who satisfies (7) in *FFVII* is not identical to the individual who satisfies (7) in *FF Tactics*. This is because the referent of "Cloud Strife" in *FF Tactics* has the astrological sign Aquarius, and it is not possible to be both a Leo and an Aquarius.

The failure of Russell's descriptivism to determine which definite description out of many is *the one* associated with a proper name has led philosophers such as John Searle (1932–) to question Russell's theory.[4] The problem Searle recognized is that for any particular utterance of a proper name, there has to be some particular definite description that the speaker has *in mind*. A moment's reflection will show that there are many possible definite descriptions, even when we stay within one *FF* world. Take the name "Tidus" from *FFX*. The definite description could be "the rising blitzball star from the Zanarkand Abes," "the son of Jecht," "the guardian of the Summoner Yuna who looks like Shuyin," or many others. This leads to two problems. First, often when we use a proper name, we have no particular definite description in mind—we are thinking of a general set of descriptions. Second, the speaker and the listener might have different definite descriptions in mind. This is a problem, because you might mean one thing when your utterance contains the name "Tidus," while I think you mean something else because I have associated a different definite description with "Tidus."

An additional objection to Russell's account comes from Saul Kripke (1940–).[5] Consider the following example to get the gist of Kripke's objection. Imagine that we are in Spira, and the Summoner Braska is on his pilgrimage to defeat Sin. In our Spira, however, Braska does not defeat Sin. Rather, before Braska can begin the summoning of his Final Aeon to defeat Sin, Schmidt defeats Sin instead but dies mysteriously afterward, without anyone learning that it was he who brought about the Calm.[6] The Summoner Braska uses the situation to his advantage and deceives the whole of Spira into believing that he defeated Sin. Obsessed with fame and glory, Braska ends his own life in order to keep up the deception that he and his Aeons brought about the Calm. His success in this trickery garners him the accolade of High Summoner, a title posthumously given only to individuals who defeat Sin.

Now, most Spirans know Braska as *the fifth High Summoner* and therefore associate the name "Braska" with the definite description "the fifth High Summoner."[7] It should also be clear that when they utter the name "Braska," they successfully refer to Braska and not to the unknown Schmidt. This is a counterexample to Russell's claim that a name refers in virtue of that referent satisfying a definite description associated in some way with the name. For, in this case, we have a name, "Braska," associated with the definite description "the fifth High Summoner," and the referent of "Braska" is not Schmidt, even though it is Schmidt who satisfies the definite description of "the fifth High Summoner."

Cloud's Link to Sephiroth and Kripke's Causal-Historical Theory

Given the problems that face Russell's descriptivist theory of reference, Kripke developed another account of how proper names come to refer, thinking specifically about how we use names in counterfactual situations (those situations that did not happen in the actual world but that could have, had particular states of affairs been different).[8] When we ask the question, "What if Cloud Strife never defeated Sephiroth?" are we talking about the same individual we know from *FFVII*, only in the situation where he didn't defeat Sephiroth, or are we identifying a completely different individual with the same name who did not defeat Sephiroth? Kripke thinks that most of us believe the former: we are all thinking of the familiar individual, but in this scenario, he did not defeat Sephiroth. This leads Kripke to claim that proper names are rigid designators—they refer to the same individual across all possible counterfactual states of affairs of which we can conceive.

Why is this problematic for Russell's descriptivism? Well, if proper names are rigid designators, then it follows that names cannot offer the same semantic contribution to sentences that definite descriptions can. Contrary to proper names, most definite descriptions are understood as *flaccid designators*, or descriptions that *do not* refer to the same referent in every possible counterfactual state of affairs of which we can conceive. Take, for example, the definite description (1), "the Materia blade–wielding protagonist of *FFVII*." When we use (1) to pick out a referent in a counterfactual state of affairs, does it follow necessarily that we are picking out Cloud Strife? Of course, in the actual state of affairs (1) picks out Cloud Strife, but need it pick out Cloud Strife in every possible counterfactual situation? Is it not possible that Tifa Lockheart satisfied (1) instead? *What if* Cloud Strife died at a young age in Nibelheim and never went on to join SOLDIER? Can't we imagine things being so different that someone else picked up a Materia blade and ultimately defeated Sephiroth in an adventure titled *FFVII*? Of course we can, so it follows that (1) doesn't pick out the same referent in all counterfactual states of affairs.

If we have two names—or terms, for that matter—that refer to different things, then it follows that those terms mean different things. For example, if we use the terms "phoenix down" and "hi-potion" in a sentence, and we also know that "phoenix down" refers to a life-replenishing feather of a Phoenix bird, and "hi-potion" refers to a hit point–restoring drink, then we also know that the terms "phoenix down" and "hi-potion" mean different things. This amounts to saying that if two terms refer to different things, then they must mean different things. Therefore, because the name "Cloud Strife" refers to the same referent in all possible counterfactual situations and (1) does not refer to the same referent in all possible counterfactual situations, then the proper name "Cloud Strife" and (1) fail to offer the same, or even similar, semantic contributions to the sentences in which they occur, contra Russell.

If proper names are the kinds of linguistic entities that refer to the same thing in every possible counterfactual scenario, how can Kripke explain how proper names refer at all? In short, he relies on an account concerning causation through history. Names come into existence in a "dubbing ceremony," the occasion where an individual is first referred to by the name. A name refers to an individual if it can be traced back through a causal-historical chain that originated with a dubbing ceremony. Let's consider a *Final Fantasy* example. Imagine that a baby is born in the small mountain village of Nibelheim, and his parents name him and subsequently refer to him by the name "Cloud Strife." The people of Nibelheim are members of a community of speakers who use the name "Cloud Strife" to refer to the child because, over time and through communication originating with his parents, they have passed the name from person to person. Due to this "name transference" from person to person and the fact that such transference ultimately leads back to the original dubbing ceremony by the parents, the name "Cloud Strife" refers to Cloud Strife.[9] For Kripke, all proper names refer to the referents they do because of a similar causal-historical chain among a community of speakers—no definite description need be associated with the name in order to successfully refer. The minor role that definite descriptions play in Kripke's theory of referring is not to *determine the referent* of a proper name, but only to help *fix the referent* in cases where the referent is not present.

Again, we must inquire into what Kripke's causal-historical theory of referring has to say about the relationship between referents who share a proper name across *FF* worlds. Recall that our intuitions for the proper name "Cid" are that no special relation holds between the referents, whereas the proper name "Cloud Strife" has referents related through identity. Only when two causal-historical chains are grounded in the same dubbing ceremony do the names transferred in the causal-historical chain have identical referents. In the case of the name "Cid," the referents who share the name across *FF* worlds will be the same referent if, and only if, they are grounded in the same naming ceremony. It is quite clear that none of the referents of the proper name "Cid" share histories, let alone dubbing ceremonies. Presumably, Cid, the King of Lindblum, and Cid, the pilot of the *Highwind*, were given the name "Cid" in very different dubbing ceremonies. Therefore, Kripke's causal-historical theory of referring squares with our intuitions that the referents of "Cid" across the *FF* worlds are unrelated.

For the name "Cloud Strife," it would seem that the referent in *FFVII* has a history similar to the referent in *FF Tactics*. For example, both are trained with a Materia blade, and both interact with a woman named Aeris Gainsborough. There are differences in their histories as well. Some of these differences are very important, such as their birthdays, as mentioned previously. Different histories entail different dubbing ceremonies, because this event would be just one part of an individual's history. Therefore, Kripke's causal-historical theory runs counter to our intuitions about the referents of the name "Cloud Strife" in *FFVII* and *FF Tactics*.[10]

Yuna, the character in *FFX* and *FFX2*, appears to give an endorsement of Kripke's view. You might remember that at the start of *FFX2*, Yuna sees a video of a man who looks very much like Tidus from *FFX*, whom she loved and thought was dead. After seeing this video, she begins to question whether this individual is Tidus. As a part of this questioning, Yuna and her friends attempt to track down the individual in the video and determine whether he is the same person she knew and loved in *FFX*. In investigating the history of the man in the video and trying to compare it to what she knows of Tidus, Yuna is attempting to determine whether the individuals share a causal history and, in doing so, establish his/their identity/identities.

Did Balamb Garden Move? Problems with Kripke's Causal-Historical Theory

Perhaps the most significant problem with Kripke's account is the "qua problem." It is possible that when hearing a name, someone could be *categorically mistaken* about the referent of the name. Let's consider an example from *FFVIII*. In this game, the mercenary force SeeD has a mobile headquarters called Balamb Garden. So, someone could say, "Balamb Garden has moved," and an uninformed listener could mistake the institution referenced for a person, as if this person has found a new home. Thinking that "Balamb Garden" names a person who has changed residences, the speaker's further uses of the name "Balamb Garden" will be categorically mistaken. In other words, instead of using the name to talk about an institution, this speaker is, mistakenly, using the name to talk about a person. And persons fall in a different category of things than institutions. Given this mistake, our intuitions say that the individual fails to refer to Balamb Garden, although it seems clear that he is a part of the causal-historical chain of the proper name "Balamb Garden." Therefore, being a part of the causal-historical chain of a proper name is not enough to successfully refer to the referent of the proper name. One response to this problem is to require a definite description to be associated with the name in mind. Regarding this example, a definite description could be "the mercenary force begun by Cid and Edea Kramer, located on the continent of Balamb." But such a response would be a mild concession to descriptivist theories of reference, certainly not in the spirit of Kripke's causal-historical account.

Where Do We Go from Here?

Neither theory fully captures our intuitions surrounding the proper names "Cid" and "Cloud Strife." So, where do we go from here? Has this philosophical discussion been a waste of time? Can we really hope for a theory of referring that squares with all of our intuitions? In all likelihood, some kind of synthesis of descriptivism and a causal-historical theory may be closer to the complete theory of reference that philosophers of language are seeking. We need to achieve a "reflective equilibrium" between our theory and our ordinary intuitions. In other words, our theory must be revised in light of our intuitions, and our intuitions must be revised in light of our theory. Although neither is free from problems, the descriptivist theory and the causal-historical theory provide the starting components in formulating a unified theory of reference that can enter into a reflective equilibrium with intuition. What must be realized is that in philosophy, starting in the right place can be just as difficult as finishing in the right place, and surely no one would think that starting is a waste of time.

NOTES

1. We would like to thank Ruth Tallman for her helpful comments on previous drafts of this chapter.

2. A British-born philosopher, whose most well known contribution to philosophy was the coauthored work *Principia Mathematica* with Alfred North Whitehead. Russell offered a rigorous philosophical analysis of the definite article *the*, which he used in order to offer accounts of how names refer and the semantic contribution names make to the sentences in which they occur.

3. Russell had another argument for names being abbreviations of definite descriptions. Consider if someone were to hear you utter the name "Cloud Strife." How would you reply if the person asked who Cloud Strife was? You might say, "The Materia blade–wielding protagonist of *Final Fantasy VII*." This amounts to saying that in everyday, common usage, what we mean when we say a proper name is simply a definite description.

4. An American-born philosopher who has made numerous contributions to both the philosophy of language and the philosophy of mind. He is currently tenured at UC Berkeley. Searle critiqued Russell's descriptivism not in order to supplant it, but to offer a modified descriptivist theory.

5. An American-born philosopher and logician who has had an enormous impact in numerous areas of philosophy, including metaphysics, epistemology, logic, and the philosophy of language. He is currently professor emeritus at Princeton University. Kripke's thorough critique of all descriptivist accounts, including Searle's modified version, gave him a clear path to offer a separate and radically different theory of reference.

6. In the world of *Final Fantasy X*, the Summoner is supposed to perish after defeating Sin, but let's pretend that the death of the Summoner Schmidt is not the orthodox death of a Summoner.

7. The past of Spira is still the same in this fictional telling, as Yunalesca, Gandof, Ohalland, and Yocun were awarded the title High Summoner for defeating Sin before Schmidt.

8. What exactly are counterfactual situations? Simply, they are hypothetical scenarios where the facts of these states of affairs are contrary to the actual state of affairs, the actual facts. Talking about counterfactuals is like talking about what the world could be like or what the world would be like if different events transpired.

9. Of fundamental importance to Kripke's account is the transference of the name from person to person, but not just any kind of name transference will do. He added a requirement in order for an utterance of a name to successfully refer. In *Naming and Necessity*, Kripke said, "When the name is 'passed from link to link,' the receiver of the name must . . . intend when he learns it to use it with the same reference as the man from whom he heard it" (Saul Kripke, *Naming and Necessity* [Cambridge, MA: Harvard University Press, 1980], p. 96).

10. In this case, however, we might want to admit that our intuitions are wrong, because clearly two individuals cannot be the same person if they have different histories. The identity of two objects entails that these objects share every property, and differing histories result in differing properties.

CONTRIBUTORS

Party Menu

Robert Arp is a Summoner, not a chick Summoner like Sarah Fisk, but a dude Summoner who moonlights as a research associate through the New York State Center of Excellence in Bioinformatics & Life Sciences, Buffalo.

Michel S. Beaulieu is a Warrior who has lost his way, and, although he teaches history and is the co-director of the Lakehead Social History Institute at Lakehead University, all of his best weapons have yet to be discovered. His attempts to level up include the books *The Lady Lumberjack: An Annotated Collection of Dorothea Mitchell's Writings* (2005) and *Essays in Northwestern Ontario Working Class History* (2008).

Jason P. Blahuta is a Summoner who married his Final Fantasy and is an associate professor of philosophy at Lakehead University. When he is not researching Machiavelli, Asian philosophy, or applied ethics, he is raising two Black Mages and is trying—unsuccessfully—to train a Shih Tzu–Moogle crossbreed in the art of nonelemental magic.

Benjamin Chandler is a Summoner who has just completed a creative writing PhD at Flinders University, Australia. His research involves heroic literature and modern fantasy from Japan and the West, so he gets to spend a lot of time reading graphic novels, watching cartoons, and playing video games. Oh, and writing fantasy novels. Who needs a Buster Sword when you've got Bahamut Zero and the Knights of the Round on your side?

Sarah Fisk is a Summoner and a PhD candidate in the Interdisciplinary Humanities Department at Florida State University. She doesn't think she would be very good at wielding a sword but can cast some amazing spells.

Kevin Fitzpatrick is an unsent White Mage trying to hold off the Farplane until he can determine whether life is worth living. In another reality, he is a PhD candidate in philosophy at Bowling Green State University, whose research interests include political philosophy, applied ethics, and epistemology.

Jay Foster aspires to be a high-level Geomancer with a devastating whirlpool limit break that could be used not only to bring academic meetings to a quick close, but also as a definitive reply to those who doubt global climate change. He received his training in the history and philosophy of science at the University of Toronto, teaches in the Department of Philosophy at Memorial University of Newfoundland, and has coedited a collection of essays on natural capital models for the journal *Environmental Monitoring and Assessment*. At the moment he is attempting to improve his job level (actually, any job would do).

David Hahn is currently a young Rogue still looking for his rat's tail so he can join the circle of Sages near all of those mountains. He staves off boredom during long airship rides by reading political and classical philosophy.

Greg Littmann is a Cactaur who teaches philosophy at Southern Illinois University in Edwardsville. He particularly likes metaphysics, moral philosophy, the philosophy of logic, and giving strangers the 1,000 needles. He plays too many computer games.

Nicolas Michaud is a Black Mage who teaches philosophy at the University of North Florida and Jacksonville University. He uses this as a cover for his true mission: training his minions to help him take over the world.

Jonah Mitropoulos is a hybrid-class Red Geomancer, fusing the Red Mage with the Geomancer. This way, he can take a holistic approach to caring for the environment. He is currently pursuing his master's degree at the University of Connecticut in the field of English.

Alex Nuttall holds a master's in philosophy from Purdue University. Alex is currently working on refining his sensibilities by exposing himself to a multitude of quality movies, games, graphic novels, music, and TV shows. In order to alter time to allow him these pursuits, he has begun studying as a Time Mage. He'll cast Immobilize, *then* Haste.

Kylie Prymus lacks the ability to wield even the most basic weapon and has been forced to abandon his aspirations of one day becoming an Onion Knight. He is currently developing his inner chi as a Monk, while teaching at Converse College and completing a dissertation on virtue theory and the Internet from Duke University, titled "Virtual Virtue." Though it rarely works, he prefers to tell everyone that he is putting off finishing his PhD because if he levels up, so will the monsters!

Andrew Russo is a White Mage—curing the wounds caused by the Cartesian influence on our language. Those in his speech community refer to him with the proper name "Andrew Russo," and he is a second-year PhD candidate at the University of Oklahoma. His main area of interest is the philosophy of mind, specifically in regard to intentionality and the way a complete philosophy of the mind should be informed by evolutionary psychology.

Jason Southworth uses the Sphere Grid, so, unlike the other contributors to this volume, he has no class (look, a double entendre). His status includes being an ABD graduate student at the University of Oklahoma, Norman, and an adjunct instructor of philosophy at Fort Hays State University, Hays, Kansas. He has contributed articles to several pop culture and philosophy volumes, including *Batman and Philosophy*, *Heroes and Philosophy*, *Stephen Colbert and Philosophy*, *X-Men and Philosophy*, and *Supervillains and Philosophy*.

Christopher Wood assures us (although his uniform may be gray and his eyes aglow) that he holds no affiliation whatsoever with the Shinra corporation, despite holding a master's in philosophy from Brock University. His research interests include contemporary continental philosophy, Asian philosophy, the history of philosophy, and aesthetics.

INDEX

Game Tips

Advent Children, 128, 132, 134
  Lifestream concept in, 49–53
  objectification in, 72–73
  viewers' passivity in, 16–17
Aeris Gainsborough, in *Final Fantasy VII*, 14, 136
  convergence under, 138–139
  nihilism of, 173
  virtues of, 79, 81
afterlife
  effects of belief in, 155–156, 172
  as goal of religion, 153–154
Age of Enlightenment, 24–25
Aizawa Seishisai, 133–134, 141n14
Aki Ross, in *The Spirits Within*, 61, 63–67
"Alternative Possibilities and Moral Responsibility" (Frankfurt), 115–117
altruism, *vs.* self-interest, 88–92
  of characters, 93–95, 97–98, 105–106
  in maximizing happiness, 96–97
  of players, 95–96, 102
anthropocentric worldviews, 67–70
apocalypse, 23–24, 47
Aquinas, Thomas, 113
Aristotle, 74
  on morality, 81, 102–105, 107
  on objectification, 81–82

art
  attention to details in, 37–38
  experience viewing, 38–39, 43
  in *Final Fantasy* series, 44
  judging quality of, 35, 38–43
  perceptions of, 37
  quality of, 33–35
  relation to morality, 41–42
authenticity, Cloud's, 177–184
authority
  characters' missions against, 95, 125–126, 145–147
  Hobbes on, 89, 93, 96
  rule-breaking by players, 96
  slave *vs.* master morality and, 29–32
autonomy, 75–78, 82
AVALANCHE, 53, 92
  destruction of Mako reactors by, 10–11, 173
  Shinra *vs.*, 49–50, 53, 143–144

Bacon, Francis, 64
Barret Wallace, in *Final Fantasy VII*, 136–137, 173
Barthes, Roland, 6, 9, 16
Bartz, in *Final Fantasy V*, 91
beauty, perceptions of, 34, 37
Beyond Good and Evil (Nietzsche), 157
biology, and personality, 119–121

Black Mages, in *Final Fantasy IX*, 186, 189

Blade Runner, 47

Braska, in *Final Fantasy VII*, 201–202

Calm, in *Final Fantasy X*, 151–153

capitalism
  in *Final Fantasy VII*, 134, 150
  invading Japan, 133–135
  Shinra compared to, 134, 137
  See also class struggle

Captain Gray, in *The Spirits Within*, 66–67

causal-historical theory, of names, 203–206

Cetra (Ancients), 131

Chappu, in *Final Fantasy X*, 153

character
  choice of, 82–83, 108
  moderation as virtue in, 103, 105
  morality based on, 80–81

characters
  Aristotle's opinion of, 104–105
  customization of, 13–14, 17–18
  evolution of, 14, 178–181
  of *Final Fantasy VII*, 167–168, 170
  of *Final Fantasy XI Online*, 93–95, 99–100, 106–107
  frivolity of, 100–101
  identification with, 18
  intelligence of, 104–105
  morality of, 97, 99–100, 106–107
  multiple playable, 6, 12–13
  players' identification with, 12–14
  proper functions of, compared to humans', 103–104
  relation to authority, 93, 95
  self-interest *vs.* altruism of, 75, 89–91, 97–98, 105–106

signifiers of, 6–8, 15–16
virtues of, 97, 105

Chocobo races, 100

Cid, in *The Spirits Within*, 54
  on fighting Phantoms, 61–62, 65–67
  on Gaia, 55–56, 58–60

Cid, name used in many games, 26, 195, 199, 204–205

class struggle
  in *Final Fantasy*, 143, 149
  morality and, 157–158, 161
  values of nobility *vs.* peasants, 29–30, 157–158

Cloud Strife, as same person in two games, 195, 200–201
  definite description of, 197–198, 200

Cloud Strife, in *Final Fantasy VII*, 131, 136, 149
  authenticity of, 177–184
  compared to Superman, 35–36
  evolution of character, 105, 178–184
  female companion of, 175
  goals of, 127, 130
  identity crisis of, 12, 134
  mystery about, 168, 174
  name as rigid designator of, 202–205
  players' identification with, 10–12
  preset signifiers of, 10, 12
  reinterpretation of, 16
  relation to the world, 170–171
  self-interest *vs.* altruism of, 90, 92
  as SOLDIER, 177, 179–182

Cloud Strife, in *Final Fantasy VIII*, 81

conceptual analysis, 49

A Contribution to the Critique of Political Economy (Marx), 144
Crisis Core, reinterpretation of signifiers in, 15–16
Crystal Chronicles, 38
cultural invasion
  in *Final Fantasy VII*, 132–136
  of Japan, 132–137
  responses to, 136–138

death
  fear of, 188–189, 191–194
  in *Final Fantasy IX*, 185–187
  morality and, 187–188
Descartes, René, 57–58, 64
descriptivism, 196–203, 206
direct reference theory, of names, 196–202, 206
Dirge of Cerberus, 17–18
The Discourses (Machiavelli), 159
Dostoyevsky, Fyodor, 28

Ecce Homo (Nietzsche), 157
ecology
  apocalypse and, 47
  Gaia concept in, 50, 54–56
  organicist concepts in, 59–60
Ellone, in *Final Fantasy VIII*, 74–75
Emperor, in *Final Fantasy VI*, 149
energy
  from Lifestream, 47–48
  spirit and *kami*, 129–130
environment
  anthropocentric worldviews *vs.*, 67–69
  apocalypse and, 47
  Final Fantasy VII as ecological metaphor, 48, 125–126, 129, 132

human damage to, 48–49, 69–71
human interactions with, 63–67, 131
in Shinto spirituality, 130, 132, 136
Epicurus, 190–193
Essay on the Principle of Population (Malthus), 69
existentialism, 25, 168–169, 174
  in *Final Fantasy VII*, 183
  godlessness of, 171–172
  Kefka's, 25, 27–28
  nihilism *vs.*, 28
  responsibility in, 177–178

Final Fantasy: The Spirits Within. See The Spirits Within
Final Fantasy series
  bad or ambiguous endings in, 146
  Cid, name used in many games in, 195, 199, 204–205
  class struggle in, 143–144
  connections among, 38–39, 195
  Final Fantasy VII in development of, 167
  good qualities of, 36–37
  political structure of society in, 146, 148–149
  popularity of, 87–88
  quality of art in, 33, 44
  solo games *vs. Final Fantasy XI Online*, 93–94
  violence in, 105, 128
Final Fantasy universe, multiple avenues into, 6, 14, 16–17
Final Fantasy I, 40
Final Fantasy III, 144
Final Fantasy VI, 24, 91

Final Fantasy VII, 79, 183
  capitalism in, 134–135
  characters in, 6, 13, 18
  cinematography of, 130,
    172–173
  compared to *Superman 64*, 35–36
  ecological concepts in, 47, 49,
    57, 125, 129
  ecoterrorists in, 125–126
  nihilism in, 172–173, 183
  Shinto spirituality in,
    126–129, 132
  specialness of, 43, 167–168
Final Fantasy VIII, 74–75, 77–79
Final Fantasy IX, 73–74,
    185–187
Final Fantasy X, 205
Final Fantasy X-2, 75, 205
Final Fantasy XI Online
  morality of characters in,
    106–107
  players of, 95–96, 99–102
  solo games *vs.*, 93–94
Final Fantasy Tactics Advance, 13
Final Fantasy VII: Advent Children.
    See Advent Children
fossil fuels, Mako's similarity to,
    48–49
Foucault, Michel, 22–24, 26, 28
Four Warriors of Light. *See* Light
    Warriors
Frankfurt, Harry, 115–117
freedom, 173–176, 178
free will
  of Heroes, 110–114
  predestination *vs.*, 117–121
  responsibility from, 175–178,
    183–184

Gage, Phineas, 120–121
Gaia, 8, 75
  Dr. Cid on, 58, 61–62

in *Final Fantasy*, 49–50,
    62–63, 74
  Lifestream concept and, 54,
    56–60
  vital principles of, 57–58
"the Gaia hypothesis," 54–58,
    62–63, 67–71
game, the
  efforts to beat, 11, 15
  incentives to finish, 14
  Superman 64 as broken, 36
gamers
  vs. players, 11
  See also players
Garland, in *Final Fantasy IX*, 74,
    115–117, 121
  on memories as eternal,
    188–189
Gee, James Paul, 7
God, in predestination *vs.* free will,
    112–113
Guardian Forces (GFs), 77–78

happiness
  death and, 191–193
  maximizing, 73, 78, 96–97
  objective value of, 190, 192
Harootunian, Harry, 133–134
Heidegger, Martin, 138, 169, 170
Hein, in *The Spirits Within*, 61
  on Gaia, 56, 58–59
  on nature and environment,
    63–65
Heroes
  Kefka *vs.*, 26–28, 31–32
  lack of thanks for, 121
  missions of, 145–147
  predestination of, 110–114,
    117–119
  self-interest *vs.* altruism, 90–93,
    97–98
  social change efforts of, 147, 149

history
    individuals' ability to change,
        144–145
    Marx on, 144, 149–150
    of names, 204–205
Hobbes, Thomas
    on authority, 89, 93, 96
    on self-interest, 88–93, 95
Hojo
    in *Final Fantasy VII*, 74, 131
    in *The Spirits Within*, 56–57, 135
holism *vs.* organicism, 51–54,
        56–58
homeostatic systems, Gaia as,
        55–56, 59, 66
Hourigan, Ben, 128
Hume, David, 37
    on art's relation to morality, 41–42
    on judging art, 33–35, 38–39,
        42–43
hypothetical imperative, 27–28

identification, of players with
        characters, 8–10, 13–16
identity statements, 196–199
Inoue Nissho, 137–138
in purification of Jenova influence,
        132
insanity
    of Kefka Palazzo, 20–22
    labels as means of control,
        22–23, 26
    linked to depravity, 24–25
    responses to, 24–25
    as veiled wisdom, 23–24
interpretations, of signifiers,
        13–14, 17–18

Japan
    allegorized, 127–128
    cultural invasion of,
        132–136, 137

kami to preserve heritage of,
        138–139
    modernization in, 127–129,
        133–134, 137
Jenkins, Henry, 8
Jenova, in *Final Fantasy VII*,
        130–132
    effects of, 129, 133, 135
    efforts to revive, 72–73
Jenova trying to take over, 131
Just War Theory, 154

Kabbalism, Sephiroth from,
        134–135
Kadaj, 131–132
Kafka, 20
kami concept, in Shinto spirituality,
        129–131, 134–135, 138–139
Kant, Immanuel, 24, 73, 76–78
Kantians, 79, 81–82
Kasulis, Thomas, 129–130
Kazushige Nojima, 53
Kefka Palazzo, in *Final Fantasy
        VI*, 24, 149
    existentialism of, 25, 27–28
    experimentation on, 21–22
    madness of, 20–22, 25–26, 31
    metamorphosis of, 26–27
    relationship with humanity and
        Moogledom, 29–30
    struggle against, 26–27, 31–32
    as Übermensch, 30–31
Kripke, Saul, 201–205
Kuja, in *Final Fantasy IX*,
        73–74, 189
    destroying source of life,
        192–193
    Vivi Orunitia created by,
        185–186

labels, influence of, 23
Large, Stephen, 137

Leviathan (Hobbes), 89
Lifestream concept, 47–49, 53–55
  compared to *kami*, 138–139
  Gaia and, 56–60
  literal *vs.* metaphorical descriptions of, 50–52
Light Warriors, 91
  ability to change society, 146–147
  predestination of, 110–114, 118–119
Lovelock, James, 50, 54–58, 62–63, 67–71
Lucretia, in *Final Fantasy VII*, 135–136
Lukahn, in *Final Fantasy I*, 110, 112–114

Machiavelli, Niccolò
  political writings of, 151–152, 160–161
  on religion, 153–154, 159, 160–161
Mad Max, 47
Madness and Civilization (Foucault), 22–23, 26
magic, 26, 32, 48
  control of, 21, 24
  technology *vs.*, 21–22
Mako reactors, 10–11, 48, 125, 131, 170, 173
Malthus, Thomas, 69
Margulis, Lynn, 50, 54–58, 62–63, 67–71
Marlboro, the, 33
Marlene Wallace, in *Advent Children*, 50–53
Marx, Karl
  on history, 144–145
  on proletariat, 142–143
  on social change, 146, 149–150

master-slave relationships, 30–31, 81, 157–158
meaning, 27, 187
  lacking for Kefka, 21, 27, 31
  learning to live without, 32, 172
  source of, 192–193
mechanism. *See* reductionism *vs.* mechanism
memories, as eternal, 188–190
Middle Ages, insanity in, 23
Midgar, in *Final Fantasy VII*, 172–173
Mill, John Stuart, 73, 96–97, 100–102
mini-quests, 9–10
MMORPG, *Final Fantasy XI Online* as, 93–94
modernization
  in Japan, 127–129, 133–134, 137
  Shinto spirituality on, 128–129
monsters/WEAPONS, choice of battling or not, 9–10
Moogles, as true proletarians, 147
morality
  action-based *vs.* character-based, 80–81
  Aristotle on, 102–108
  art's relation to, 41–42
  class struggle and, 157–158, 161
  development of concept of good and evil in, 29–30
  ethical decision making, 79
  of *Final Fantasy* characters, 106–107
  of *Final Fantasy* players, 95–96, 99–102, 107–108
  immorality and, 72–74
  inconsistencies in *Final Fantasy* series, 75–76
  inversion of, 157
  knowledge in, 188
  maximizing happiness as, 96–97

moderation in, 103, 105, 107
need to decide own values,
173–177
Nietzsche on, 28–30, 152, 172
of nobility *vs.* peasants, 29–30,
157–158
on objectification, 73–74, 77–79
rational justifications for, 24
responsibility in, 10–11, 23–25,
175–177
sacrifice of innocents in utilitarianism, 79–80
self-interest *vs.* altruism in,
88–92
of slave *vs.* master, 30–31, 81
utilitarian, 78–80
of Vivi Orunitia, 187–188

names
causal-historical theory of,
203–206
direct reference theory of,
196–202, 206
intuitions about, 195, 206
as rigid designators, 202–205
significance of, 195–196, 201
nature
in Shinto spirituality, 126–127
technology *vs.*, 138–139, 156
See also environment
Necron, in *Final Fantasy IX*,
192–193
New Theses (Seishisai), 133
Nicomachean Ethics (Aristotle), 102
Nietzsche, Friedrich, 153
existentialism of, 28, 168–169
on morality, 28–30, 152, 157
on religion, 151, 155–156,
161–162, 171–172
on Übermensch, 30–31
virtue ethics of, 81–82
nihilism, 31

existentialism *vs.*, 28
in *Final Fantasy VII*,
172–173, 183

objectification
in *Advent Children*, 72–73
moral theories on, 73–74, 79,
81–82
permission to be used in, 74–77
On Bullshit (Frankfurt), 115
On the Genealogy of Morals
(Nietzsche), 28–30, 157
organicism. *See* holism *vs.*
organicism

perceptions, relation to objects'
qualities, 37
Phantoms, 59, 61, 63–67
philosophy, analysis of concepts
in, 49
places, signifiers of, 9
players
customization of characters by,
7–8, 13
of *Final Fantasy XI Online*,
95–96, 99–102
gamers *vs.*, 11
identification with characters,
8–14
morality of, 99–102, 107–108,
144
PlayStation, new capabilities of,
167
politics, religion serving, 159–161
The Politics (Aristotle), 104
power
Heroes' missions against,
145–146
as highest virtue, 75, 81
responsibility for actions outside
our own, 113–118
See also authority

praise
for biologically influenced
personality, 120–121
for predestined actions,
111–112, 118–119
predestination. *See* free will
prequels, 15
Princess Ashe, in *Final Fantasy
XII*, 93
procreation, and fear of death,
189–190
proletariat, 142–143, 147
purification rituals, 132, 135–136

Queen Brahne, in *Final Fantasy IX*,
73–74
"The Question Concerning
Technology" (Heidegger),
138

Rat Kid, in *Final Fantasy IX*, 142
readers, in production of text,
6, 18
reason, 24, 31, 76, 103
in judging art, 39–41
Kefka's excess of, 25–26
reductionism *vs.* mechanism,
52–53, 55–60
religion, 42, 160
abolition of, 32, 161–162,
171–172
anthropocentric worldviews
in, 67
death of God, 28–31
development of concept of evil
in, 29–30
effects of, 151–153
effects of belief in heaven,
155–157, 172
existentialism on, 171–172
in *Final Fantasy X*, 151, 153

Japan's fear of Christianity,
133–134
serving political purposes, 154,
159–161
values of nobility *vs.* peasants in,
157–158
veracity of, 158–159, 161
responsibility
for biologically influenced
personality, 120–121
in existentialism, 177–178,
183–184
from free will, 175–178
moral, 10–11, 23–25
for predestined actions, 113–119
rigid designators, names as,
202–205
Rome, religion serving political
purposes in, 160
Ross, Floyd Hiat, 129–130
RPGs
party-based *vs.* strategy-based,
12–13
players' identification with
characters in, 11–12
popularity of, 87–88
Russell, Bertrand, 196–202, 203

sacrifice
by *Final Fantasy* characters,
79, 90
of self, 80
of Summoners, 155–156, 161
in utilitarianism, 75, 79–80
Yuna refusing, 155
Yuna's, 78–79, 92
Sakaguchi Hironobu, 53, 126
Sartre, Jean-Paul
existentialism of, 28, 169
on paradox of freedom, 174–176
on self-deception, 176–177

Savonarola, 159
Scipio Africanus, 160
Searle, John, 201
Sector 7 slums, in *Final Fantasy VII*, 11, 149
Seifer, in *Final Fantasy VIII*, 81
self-interest. *See* altruism, *vs.* self-interest
semiology, 6
Sephiroth, in *Final Fantasy VII*, 134–136, 149
  Cloud *vs.*, 90, 92, 182
  viciousness of, 74, 81
Shinra Corporation, in *Final Fantasy VII*, 127, 149
  assassination of president of, 137–138
  AVALANCHE *vs.*, 49–50, 53, 90
  classism of, 143–144
  compared to capitalism, 134, 137
  objectifying Gaia, 75, 125
Shinto: The Way Home (Kasulis), 129
Shinto: The Way of Japan (Ross), 129
Shinto spirituality
  essentialist, 134, 136, 138
  in *Final Fantasy VII*, 126–129, 132, 138–139
  kami concept in, 129–131, 134–135
  on modernization, 128–129
  State, 134
  tsumi concept in, 130–136
signifiers
  of *Final Fantasy* characters for gamers *vs.* players, 11
  interpretations of, 6, 9–10, 17–18
  preset, 6–7, 9, 12–13
  reinterpretation of, 12, 15–16
  sources of, 8–9
  in writerly *vs.* nonwriterly texts, 17–18
Sin, in *Final Fantasy X*, 151, 156–157
  defeat of, 155, 201–202
  unable to be destroyed, 152, 158–159, 161
  Yuna *vs.*, 92–93
social contract, 89, 96
society, 173
  Heroes' ability to change in, 146–147, 149
  individuals' ability to change, 144–145
  political structure of, 146–149
  roles within, 176–177
SOLDIER, Cloud as, 177, 179–182
Spira, in *Final Fantasy X*
  desire for Calm, 152–153
  religion in, 151, 160, 162
  role of Summoners in, 156
The Spirits Within, 16, 70
  Gaia and the environment in, 56–66
  Lifestream in, 49, 53–60
Squall Leonhart, in *Final Fantasy VIII*, 74–75, 92, 105
  as Leon in *Kingdom Hearts I* and *II*, 196, 198–199
Square Enix corporation, control of *Final Fantasy XI Online* by, 96
Suikoden, as party-based and strategy-based, 13
Summoners, in *Final Fantasy X*

Summoners (*continued*)
  blamed for Sin, 158
  dependence on, 153, 156, 158
  goals of, 152–153
  religion of, 151
  sacrifice of, 155–156, 161
  sending spirits to Farplane, 159
Superman 64, compared to *Final
    Fantasy VII*, 35–36

technology
  magic *vs.*, 21–22
  nature *vs.*, 138–139, 156
  rejected in *Final Fantasy X*, 153,
    156, 158
Terra Branford, in *Final Fantasy VI*,
    148–149
text
  created through players' identifi-
    cation, 11
  different perspectives on, 13
  writerly, 7, 14, 16–18
Theses on Feurebach (Marx), 145
Tidus, in *Final Fantasy X* and *X-2*,
    78, 92, 205
  goals of, 152–153
  self-interest *vs.* altruism of, 90
Tifa, in *Final Fantasy VII*,
    178–179, 181
Treatise of Man (Descartes), 57–58
tsumi concept, in Shinto spiritual-
    ity, 132–138

Übermensch, Kefka as, 30–31
utilitarianism, 78–80
  inconsistencies in *Final Fantasy*
    series, 75–76
  on objectification, 81–82
Utilitarianism (Mill), 97

Vaan, in *Final Fantasy XII*, 144

values
  choosing, 194
  of nobility *vs.* peasants, 29–30,
    157–158
  objective, 190, 192–193
  Vivi Orunitia's, 187–190, 193
Vana'diel, characters' proper
    functions on, 103–104
video games
  Final Fantasy I in infancy
    of, 40
  quality of art in, 34, 44
Vincent, in *Dirge of Cerberus*, 18
Vincent Valentine, in *Advent
    Children*, 131
violence, 105, 128
virtue ethics, 74–76
  Aristotle's, 103, 105
  Nietzsche's, 81
  on objectification, 81–82
  two perspectives on, 82–83
Vivi Orunitia, in *Final Fantasy
    IX*, 142
  creation of, 185–186
  on deaths, 190–191
  procreation of, 189–190
  values of, 187–188, 190, 193

Wakka, in *Final Fantasy X*,
    153, 159
Wakabayashi, Bob Tadashi, 133
worlds
  Final Fantasy's not connected,
    195
  humans' inseparability from, 169
  importance to characters,
    170, 183
writerly texts, multiple signifiers
    in, 18
Wutai, in *Final Fantasy VII*,
    127–128

Yevon, in *Final Fantasy X*, 151, 153, 155, 157, 160
   abolition of, 161–162
   based on lie, 158–159, 161
Yoshinori, Kitase, 126
Yuffie, in *Final Fantasy VII*, 127
Yuna, in *Final Fantasy X* and *X-2*, 78–79, 159–160, 205

altruism of, 92–93, 105–106, 155

Zack, in *Final Fantasy VII*, 15–16, 180, 182
Zidane Tribal, in *Final Fantasy IX*, 92